STEP INTO MY HEART

"In *Step Into My Heart*, Anthony J. Mussari brings to light his powerful experience as a patient who has been transformed by open-heart surgery. This is a book written autobiographically for the purpose of allowing other people to better understand the experience of vulnerability, hardship, survival, depression, and resiliency. A teacher by profession, Mussari is able to convey the ultimate value of love in our lives. This book is beautifully written and a gem for students of life and of the medical humanities."

—*Stephen G. Post, Ph.D.*
Division Head, Medicine in Society
Director, Center for Medical Humanities,
Compassionate Care, and Bioethics
Stony Brook University
Author, *Why Good Things Happen To Good People*

"The experiences you share in your book would be a warm, and comforting experience for all who read it, whatever their religion may be. I hope it reaches many people with its healing messages."

—*Father Joseph Girzone*
Author, the *Joshua Series*

"Like the proverbial phoenix, Tony Mussari has emerged from a devastating experience to create yet another chapter in his amazing life. He and Kitch remind us that generosity of heart can survive through great adversity. Although Tony speaks to the experience of the open-heart patient, his own "open-heart" will speak to a broad spectrum of people who seek a way to work through and triumph over adversity with grace and joy."

—*Atty. Barbara Hack*
New York, NY

"Step Into My Heart is very brave and moving. Tony Mussari's recounting of his brush with mortality resonates with emotional honesty. This is a story of personal growth, friendship and the necessity for gratitude even when confronted with terrifying adversity."
— *Dr. Caoilfhionn Ni Bheachain*, Communications
Department of Management and Marketing
Kemmy Business School, University of Limerick, Ireland

"As I read pre-publication excerpts from *Step Into My Heart*, rushing to the forefront of my mind was the thought: *The seemingly important things become trivial and the seemingly trivial things become important by the mere shifting of circumstances.* Tony Mussari has done an excellent job in figuratively "opening up his heart" as he guides readers through the physical, mental, emotional and spiritual experiences of open-heart surgery. He vividly and honestly describes his life before, during and after surgery. Tony advises, "If you don't reach out for help, you won't get it." I recommend reaching out for this book—and sharing it with those you love."
— *Carl Mays*
Author and Speaker

"Every one of us at different times in our life goes through experiences when things don't work out the way we would like. For some, this means living in turmoil, anxiety, fear and frustration. In *Step Into My Heart*, Dr. Tony Mussari provides one person's inner reflections on the battle with anxiety and depression during uncertain times with thoughtful deliberation and keen insight. He illustrates how one can cast out anxiety and fear and live a healthy, productive life even during trying times. Anyone who has ever struggled with anxiety and depression will gain strength, support and encouragement after reading the pages in this book. Dr. Mussari's words are truly inspirational and heartfelt."
— *Kristie M. Nardell, M.D.*
WVHCS, Kingston, PA

"If you want to be inspired and touched, *Step Into My Heart: Heart Disease and Open-heart Surgery, My New Best Friends*, does just that. Written by revered teacher Tony Mussari, this book not only explores the steps and challenges of open-heart surgery, but more importantly leads you on a journey of the soul. It is a stirring and inspirational trip inside the heart and mind of an extraordinary teacher and man who despite his many challenges, reveals and expresses the American spirit through the love and compassion of those around him. He shows us we can learn something new from each other when we take the time to listen."

—*Julie Marvel*
Moraga, California

"*Step Into My Heart* is appropriately titled, because that's exactly what I did—I stepped into the author's heart, for a brief visit—a chat, a laugh, a shared common bond. I too was faced with open-heart surgery in January of 2007 after suffering a heart attack. So much in these pages speaks to me directly, as if it had been written specifically for me. Tony referenced *E.T.* as well as other movies with the deft skill of a film historian, which appealed to me immediately given the fact that I grew up in the movie theatre business. These cinematic images were analogous to his life-changing experience, and in many ways mirrored my own. I am reminded as well of the similar stories told to me by others who've had the same experience. No matter if you or a loved one is facing the surgery or is recovering from it, *Step Into My Heart* speaks from the heart. In my case, I read it well after my surgery and took away from it the universal truth that all of us experience—that fear, anger, sadness, the testing of faith, and the regaining of strength is a natural process. And it's all here—told in a way that is always hopeful, courageous, and filled with the belief that life is absolutely worth living."

—*Tom Alexander*
Broadcaster/Writer/Composer
Davie, Florida

"Congratulations on your success of completing *Step Into My Heart*. From all indications it will be a healing tool in the hands of those facing and recovering from one of life's most difficult crossroads. I do believe we all have the power of healing in our hearts but it takes mortal men to educate and empower others to integrate the healing power of the mind, which you do with such simple, relatable, clarity."

—*Robin Hurt*
www.washyourhands.org

"The chapter on caregiving is the dictionary for caregivers."

—*Mrs. Louis Bigiarelli*
Caregiver, West Wyoming, PA

"WOW! Your book is going to be terrific! As always, thank you for your contribution to 'good'."

—*Chivon MacMillan*
Windsor, New Jersey

"I know one of your purposes in writing the book is to help people who are facing open-heart surgery. The rich descriptions you offer are palpable. I think your chapter about the Cardiac Intensive Care Unit, "Danger Zone," is compelling reading, both for healthcare professionals and lay people. I think potential patient and family members will be able to relate to your experience, your fears and concerns."

—*Nancy Dines, RN*
CTICU, Wilkes-Barre General Hospital

"Tony, thank you for allowing me to read some sections of your book. I realized once more how much I miss you and Kitch and your presence as colleagues.

As I read the words I thought about you and your heart as symbols of your life and love. The two things that came to my mind are its enormity and its strength. Your heart has been and is so enormous that it has been able to embrace sadness and joy, the powerful and the broken, and individuals and institutions. Your heart has been and is so strong because it has been tempered by trial and because it has been refreshed by joy. Through this book you can share this enormous and strong love with those who have not been privileged to be touched by your life."

—Margaret Monahan Hogan, Ph.D.
McNerney-Hanson Professor of Ethics
Executive Director, Garaventa Center for
Catholic Intellectual Life and American Culture
Professor of Philosophy
University of Portland

"Thanks for the entry into some passages from your book. Your story is compelling, lively, and abundantly confirmed by your wide circle of friends and the witnesses who have lived your journey to health with you.

May Our Lord always be with you and your family. That includes your Dad, the railroad man, perhaps your first guide to the turbulent passing world (Watch out, Tony, here comes that train again!)."

—Dr. Richard Loomis
Professor Emeritus
Nazareth College of Rochester

STEP INTO MY HEART

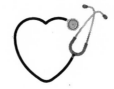

STEP INTO MY HEART

Heart Disease and Open-heart Surgery - My New Best Friends

ANTHONY J. MUSSARI, Ph.D.

Producer, Windsor Park Stories

Professor Emeritus, King's College

with

Kitch Loftus-Mussari

Foreword by Michael D. Harostock, M.D.

Chief of Cardiac Surgery

The Heart and Vascular Institute

Wilkes-Barre General Hospital

AVENTURA
PRESS

Eynon, PA

Cover and interior design by Avventura Press

ISBN-13: 978-0-9761553-5-5

Published by
Avventura Press
133 Handley St.
Eynon PA 18403-1305
570-876-5817
www.avventurapress.com

1st printing November 2008

Printed in the United States of America

For the person who saved my life,
Dr. Michael Harostock

And the person who makes life worthwhile,
Kitch

A day of celebration with doctors and friends
three months after surgery.

The collage for our Heart Scene *series.*

Family, friends, and members of my
medicalteam present the last episode of our
Heart Scene *series to WBRE TV*

CONTENTS

FOREWORD
Quintessence

Dr. Anthony Mussari is quintessence.

As a teacher he embodies the altruism of his profession. Always teaching, always asking with the intent of allowing the realization of the answers to focus attention on some relevance not otherwise common or obvious. Always expecting the best from his students as he always expected the best from himself. I know, I remember him from King's College, Wilkes-Barre, PA in the early 1970s.

As a patient he exhibited the textbook psyche of someone about to face one of the greatest challenges of his life. This is where the eternal student, the intense professor and the determined patient came together to transcend his retirement and create his signature work, *Heart Scene: A Journey of Discovery and Recovery* for his television series, Windsor Park Stories.

I believe his signature piece was Tony Mussari, rejuvenated, exercising daily, growing stronger, realizing his potential, and no longer fearing to be himself.

I proudly watched as a frightened man walked away from the hospital after open-heart surgery not knowing what life to expect from life. And I proudly watched as he worked to regain his strength and endurance and take back his life and provide that which he has done for so many years and for so many people, teach.

He taught himself to take time for himself. He taught others not to be afraid of the uncertain.

Looking through the viewfinder of his camera he captured open-heart surgery experiences that show the world in explicit technical detail (as his wife Kitch says, "with viewer discretion advised") the concerted effort of many people all with different skill sets. Now through his words he lets you follow his thinking throughout the process.

For me, Dr. Mussari's story is a valuable community resource.

He and his wife have told their story in a way that resonates with other open-heart patients. I refer many patients and families to their *Heart Scene* series archived at windsorparktheater.com. They are most appreciative of this resource. After viewing the episodes they often say to me: "Now I know what you do."

This book will be another resource that will help patients, family members, and friends better understand what goes on in the mind, heart and soul of an open-heart patient. It will help to explain aspects of the recovery process that are seldom discussed.

This is not a medical book. It is a human story about a patient's journey before and after cardiac surgery. It will give people hope, because it is a roadmap for a healthy heart and a healthy life.

It is another example of Tony Mussari, the teacher, sharing what he knows to help others learn and grow.

Michael D. Harostock, MD
Chief of Cardiac Surgery
The Heart and Vascular Institute
Wilkes-Barre General Hospital

INTRODUCTION

In the middle of difficulty lies opportunity.
Albert Einstein

If you read the title of this book carefully, you might be thinking: "He's lost his mind. How could heart disease and open-heart surgery be anyone's friends?" I assure you I haven't lost my mind. What I've lost are the things in my life that contributed to my coronary event and to my surgery.

To make a long story short, I am a man with heart disease and four coronary artery by-pass grafts that changed my life forever.

I am not unlike millions of people in America and around the world who have had or need to have this surgery. I am one of the lucky ones. I had it. I survived, and I am thriving because I now know how to live life in productive ways.

I can say with all honesty that my coronary event and open-heart surgery were the most positive learning experiences of my life. This is a book about what I learned, how I changed, and why I am trying to make the most of my second chance at life.

Please do not misunderstand or misinterpret my words or my intentions. I would not wish either of my new best friends on anyone. They are frightening, demoralizing, and very challenging experiences. For some people, they can be life-altering and devastating experiences.

That was the case with my brother. From childhood, he was my anchor and my best friend. Throughout our lives, we made big plans for our golden years. We wanted to visit every major league ballpark in America. We wanted to attend every Penn State football game as brothers and friends. We wanted to experience all the good things that come with retirement. It will not happen because my brother died of a heart attack in the bathroom of his hotel room shortly after he and his wife left the Blockbuster Bowl in December 1990.

If you are reading this, you may know someone like me. Maybe it's a relative, maybe it's a friend, or maybe it's you. Whatever the case, what is written here is intended to help people with the same kind of problems my brother and I had. It is my hope that the stories in the book will help people seek help and make lifestyle changes before it's too late.

In another respect, this book is designed to demystify the process of open-heart surgery and lessen the fear that most people have of this procedure. It is not a book filled with medical terminology and jargon. It is a personal story that details my experiences before, during, and after my cardiac event, the operation, and recovery. It's a teacher's story told in a teacher's way.

It is a story about causes and consequences, disappointments and opportunities, lessons learned and lessons applied. It is a story about overcoming fears and never giving up. It's a story about the destructive power of stress and the healing power of friendship. It is a story about the life-sustaining power of affirmation and gratitude. It's a story about finding peace and contentment.

On another level, this is a story about a caring, compassionate, competent surgeon, and his wonderful team. It's the story about the way my surgeon fixed my damaged heart and helped me to mend a broken heart.

It's a story about moving beyond an achievement-centered life to a life that is filled with things that really matter.

For me it's been a journey of discovery, growth, and change. I was a denier. I had symptoms of heart disease for some time, but I attributed them to the flu and anything that would keep me away from doctors and out of the hospital.

I was afraid of every step in this process.

I dismissed the suggestion of a Thallium stress test as a great inconvenience. I was afraid of the idea of a cardiac catheterization. Just thinking about someone putting an intravenous needle into a vein on the back of my hand made me queasy. For a teacher who began every semester with a lecture about fear and how to overcome it, I was not able to apply the principles I taught my students to my own medical needs.

My fears brought me very close to death.

I am not alone in this behavior. Last year one of our guests from Ireland applauded the candid comments I made about my fears at our annual Irish Teachers Festival in Windsor Park. With tears in her eyes she told me she lost her husband because he was afraid of the operation.

I am positive that stories like that are told all over the world every day of the year, and I am convinced that death need not be the only option. If you want to live a good quality, healthy life, heart disease and open-heart surgery need not create a mental block for you.

This book grows out of a twenty-one-part series my wife and I produced for our television program, *Windsor Park Stories, Heart Scene: A Journey of Discovery and Recovery*. It is the most important and challenging work we have ever done. It was made possible by the generosity of spirit and kindness of my surgeon, Dr. Michael Harostock, the support of the administration of the Wilkes-Barre General Hospital, and the cooperation of medical personnel and staff of the hospital.

The series about my open-heart journey was designed to express my gratitude to Dr. Harostock, his wife, Beverly, and the team of doctors, nurses and technicians who saved my life. It was motivated by a desire to share everything my wife, Kitch, and I learned about life, growth, happiness, kindness, friendship, fulfillment and a healthy heart lifestyle.

Joe Zimak, the person who operated the heart-lung machine during my surgery, encouraged me to move forward with this book when he spoke these words during an interview for our *Heart Scene* series: "You're going to show people that surgery is a reasonable thing to do. There are some things you have to overcome, some fears, but you're here talking to me today about this. That's all that need be said."

A dear friend and a retired teacher, Bill Gaydos, was equally encouraging when he shared this thought; "I know your *Heart Scene* series will save many lives. I think you have a book in here someplace that would be very helpful to many people."

In a very real way, Bill is the father of this book. His words, recorded in dozens of e-mails, made me believe that this was a great opportunity to help others. He convinced me that I should invite people to step into my heart to learn how the anxiety, fear, and trauma of heart disease and open-heart surgery changed my outlook on life, giving me peace of mind and a better understanding of what really is worthwhile.

Another friend, Joanne Chabalko, encouraged me to write this book. Our ten-part series about West Point brought us together. She watched the episodes because her son graduated from The United States Military Academy the year Kitch and I produced these programs as a part of our *What Is America?* series. She liked what she saw, and she became an enthusiastic supporter of Windsor Park Stories. Joanne suggested an autobiographical approach with these words: "I personally would love to hear your journey and how you arrived at all the places you did!"

Without question, the mother of this book is my wife, Kitch. Without her advice, encouragement, and editorial skills you would not be reading *Step Into My Heart*.

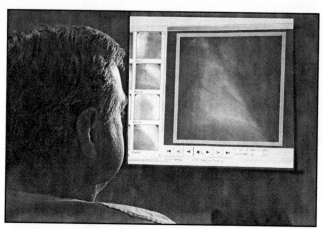

Dr. Michael Harostock studying my cardiac catheterization results

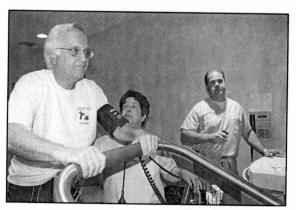

Dr. Joseph Briskie monitoring my Thallium stress test

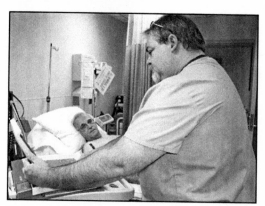

Bob Hapeman administering an EKG

LIFE DOESN'T HAPPEN
IN A VACUUM

*What everyone wants in life is continuous
and genuine happiness.*
Baruch Spinoza

When I was a youngster growing up at 27 Columbus Avenue in Coaltown, USA, better known to most people by its formal name, Wilkes-Barre, Pennsylvania, my mother would tell me more times than I wanted to hear it, "Tell me who your company is and I will tell you who you are."

It was an uncomplicated time. The Catholic Church and its parochial school was the center of our universe. Home was a place where people gathered to visit and talk. It was a clean, comfortable, welcoming place heated by anthracite coal. Oh, how I loved to watch the coal man drop two tons of coal into our coal bin. There was nothing quite like the sights and sounds of that event.

In the summer, everything took second place to the New York Yankees. We were die-hard Yankee fans. Every day began with the sports page and ended with a discussion about why the Yankees won or lost. Names like DiMaggio, Berra, Crosetti, and Rizzuto made the members of my family, especially my brother and me, feel that anything was possible in America.

For recreation, we swam in the Susquehanna River at Falls, Pennsylvania, where my grandmother had a cottage. At night, we gathered around the radio and listened to Fibber McGee and

Molly, The Green Hornet and Amos 'n' Andy. If we were good, my mother would let us stay up beyond our bedtime to hear Al Jolson sing in his unique style on the radio.

I was the youngest of three children. My brother, Ken, was the oldest. He was my hero. For years, we roomed together, and we shared an old-fashioned cast-iron bed. He had the brains in our family and the position of honor reserved for all firstborn males in Italian families. He wore this distinction well.

My sister, Mary Claire, was the beautiful and social one in our family. The older she got the more attractive she became. She always had her own room, and she loved to boss me around. I liked her, but we argued a lot. In many ways, she was as gifted as my brother.

I was the unexpected child, born during the worst year of World War II: General Douglas MacArthur was forced out of the Philippines, and he issued his famous "I shall return" promise, FDR ordered a universal draft, Japanese Americans were forced into detention camps, the Germans launched their offensive in North Africa, the infamous Battle of Bataan took place, 1,500 Jews were gassed at Auschwitz, the aircraft carrier *Lexington* was sunk, nightly "Dim Outs" began on the East Coast, food was rationed, and night baseball was banned in New York City, and that was just in the first two months of my life.

While our nation and the free world rallied around the leadership of President Franklin D. Roosevelt and the English Prime Minister, Winston Churchill, I grew up in a house that was fearful, but very patriotic. It was a scary time, and often my mother would tell us, if we were not good and we didn't behave, we might be deported. We learned early on that it was better to fit in than to stand out. It was something my mother learned in my grandmother's neighborhood store.

My mother wanted us to belong and to be respected in our neighborhood and our community. She wanted us to be American in every respect of the word as she knew it. Before the war ended,

I could sing virtually ever song that celebrated America. Most of the lyrics I remember to this day.

In grade school, I stumbled around a lot trying to find my place at home and at school. The thick wire-rimmed eyeglasses I had to wear did not make my life easier. In many respects, my glasses and my size became an invitation to any bully who wanted to prove how tough he was. I was always willing to oblige.

In those years, trouble had a way of finding me. It was not easy being the baby in a family of overachievers. It was not easy following the lead of my brother and sister. They made such a positive impression on everyone they met. I can't tell you how many times I heard these words: "Your brother and sister were excellent students. Your brother and sister were so easy to raise. Until you were three you were an angel just like your brother and sister."

My brother was a manager for the basketball team. I wanted to be a starter on the basketball team. My brother never played baseball. He just knew about everything there is to know about the game. I wanted to be a pitcher or a center fielder.

Despite our differences, he was the best friend I ever had.

I managed to graduate from high school in 1959. During my freshman year in college, I caught Kennedy fever, and to this day, I have a very special place in my heart for the 1960 presidential campaign of Senator John F. Kennedy.

The day he went to the schoolhouse in Allentown, Pennsylvania, and wrote: "Knowledge is power. Francis Bacon" on the blackboard was the day I made up my mind that my life would be spent in a classroom.

I graduated from the local Catholic college for men, King's College, in 1963. I was in the rare book room of the Erie County Public Library on November 22, 1963, the day the world stood still. After President Kennedy's assassination, I finished my masters degree at Niagara University, and then I went to Kent State University in Ohio, for two years. I got married, and I accepted a teaching position in Cedar Rapids, Iowa. There, my world changed forever.

It was 1966. America was in transition. It was a time of great change and great political unrest. It was a time of the Beatles, Bobby, Vietnam, Gene McCarthy, and Dr. Timothy Leary. In 1968, by a stroke of fate, I was right in the middle of it all. I was having the time of my life growing and doing things that shaped my thinking for the rest of my life.

I appeared on a local television program with Edward P. Morgan. After the show, the award winning newsman told me to leave the classroom and enter the newsroom.

When Senator Robert Kennedy came to Marion, Iowa, to campaign for Congressman John C. Culver, I encouraged every student I could find to make a homemade sign welcoming Senator Kennedy. He was impressed. Congressman Culver was curious, and two days later I found myself in his office talking about how I organized the welcoming party. That was my gateway into national politics.

Two years later, I was the young college teacher who by day organized college students for Robert Kennedy's primary campaigns in Nebraska and South Dakota and by night taped, lectures for his students at Mt. Mercy College in Cedar Rapids, Iowa.

Then it happened. The world stood still again. Not once, but twice. April 4, 1968, James Earl Ray killed the dreamer, Dr. Martin Luther King, Jr.; two months later, June 4, Sirhan Bishara Sirhan shot Senator Kennedy. It was a dark and lonesome time that left a permanent mark on my soul.

I went home to accept a visiting professorship at my alma mater for one year. It turned out to be a thirty-seven year journey that ended in 2005 with a project about a coach named Brooks who believed in opportunity, a miracle team that never gave up, a magic moment unrivaled in American sports and a quotation that put everything I taught about life and learning into perspective: "Impossible is just a degree of difficulty."

My world has always been a world of ideas, dreams, pictures, and relationships. I am very right-brained. I like people, and I like to do things that help and serve people. I am organic in almost everything I do. This drives structured people nuts, but it is just the way my mind works. I have been making documentaries since 1972, and you would be hard-pressed to find traditional scripts for any of these works. It was not until closed captioning for the hearing impaired became the order of the day that Kitch and I began to prepare transcripts for Windsor Park Stories, a television series we produced from 1997 to the present.

In 1996, Kitch and I built Windsor Park without an architect. There were no plans for the project. It started with an idea to reclaim a vacant and neglected parcel of land, and it grew into a garden with nine separate rooms. Since 1996, it has been the outdoor set for our TV series, *Windsor Park Stories.* The premise for the series is simple. People come to Windsor Park. They sit among the flowers in a peaceful setting, and they tell their story of hope, inspiration, and service.

If there is any one thing that defines my life, it is hard work. I learned the value of work from my parents. They both worked very hard to give their children opportunities they did not have themselves. If we wanted something, we had to work to earn the money to purchase it. There were no loans, no credit cards, and no free rides.

At age five, I helped my brother with his paper route. My mother made a special bag that enabled me to carry and deliver a few papers every afternoon. Faithfully, I tagged along with my brother who was twelve. As I got older, the bag got bigger.

What a sight that must have been! What a smart move on my mother's part! It got the both of us out of the house for about two hours every afternoon giving her some peace and quiet.

To earn the money for my first baseball glove, I cleaned out cellars, and I cashed in soda bottles that I found during the clean up. In the winter, I shoveled sidewalks for any one who would pay me fifteen cents. As I got older, I found other kinds of work. If truth be told, I quickly became a Type A workaholic. I have always had more than one job. For me that is a normal state of affairs.

My mother was serious by nature. She was a registered nurse who put her profession on hold to be a full-time mom. She kept our home and us immaculate.

She cooked, cleaned, washed, baked, and managed the family finances. She was small in stature, but an overwhelming force in our lives. A strict disciplinarian with a fixed set of rules and swift justice when those rules were broken, she expected us to behave.

She lived by a code of sayings that I can hear to this day: *Actions speak louder than words. Cleanliness is like godliness. You can't judge a book by its cover. A stitch in time saves nine. Your health is your wealth. Tell me who your company is, and I'll tell you who you are. A friend in need is a friend indeed. You make your bed, you lay in it. Waste not, want not. Don't cry over spilled milk.*

My mother was very wise in the ways of the world. The older I got the wiser she became. She demanded and received our loyalty and respect. The three of us wanted to please her at any cost.

My dad was a softer personality. His work on the Delaware and Hudson Railroad was not easy, but he loved what he did and it showed. His days were long, beginning at 5 a.m. The aroma of fresh-brewed coffee warming on a coal stove in the kitchen heralded the beginning of every day. He worked overtime whenever asked, and every payday he purchased a US Government Savings Bond in one of our names.

Over the years, my mother carefully parceled out those bonds in three groups: one group for my brother Ken, another group for my sister Mary Claire, and a third group for me. The day I made that discovery was one of the most humbling experiences of my life. It spoke volumes about who my parents were and how much they were willing to sacrifice for their children.

The World War II generation knew something about sacrifice, thrift, discipline, and doing the right thing. They passed it on to their children, and we learned quickly that the way to honor them was to make the most of our opportunities.

Whenever we had free time, my dad would take us to the round house to see steam engines being washed, or we would visit one of the railroad yards where we hitched a ride on a steam locomotive. He loved buying us ice cream in Dixie cups. He was a man with a heart of gold and a smile that radiated goodness.

Every night I would go with him to the cellar where he would open the coal bin and shovel coal into our coal furnace. Somehow that act defined masculinity for me. It also helped me to learn about politics and government.

One night my father nailed a picture of Harry Truman to the coal bin door. President Truman was one of his heroes. When Truman campaigned for reelection in 1948, my father took me to Public Square to see him. It was a defining moment for me. Sitting on my dad's shoulders so that I could see the president of the United States, I identified with his slight build and his wire rim glasses. For one of the first times in my young life, I did not feel odd. In my six-year-old brain, I reasoned that because I looked like him, I could be like him.

That was my first lesson in leadership. It captivated my imagination. I identified with the small man with glasses and spunk. He spoke his mind. I liked that quality of openness and candor, and so did my dad.

In the summer, Saturday was a special day. That was the day we walked to town with my father. In post-war America, Wilkes-Barre was a thriving city, and most people walked everywhere. Along Main Street there were vendors and "snake oil" salesmen. On Public Square, there were preachers waving bibles and screaming the message of the Lord. One of these people we knew. He was our egg man. We never paid the others much attention. We were Roman Catholics, and Sunday was our day to praise the Lord in St. Mary's Church on South Washington Street. For us, religion was a private and very solemn experience.

We attended St. Mary's, the Irish Catholic church. At that time, it was the custom to attend a church of your ethnic background, but we ended up at the Irish church thanks to a disagreement my grandmother had with the pastor of the Italian church. In those days, ethnicity was at the root of everything, and because of my grandmother's decision, we were pioneers of a sort!

When we walked to town I loved to count the movie theaters. Wilkes-Barre had six movie theaters in the central business district and others in several of the neighborhoods. My favorite was the Penn Theater. Located in the second block of Main Street, it had two balconies, and it featured live vaudeville performances.

Oh, how I loved vaudeville! As I write this, scenes from my life at the Penn Theater flash through my brain. My personal favorite is the time I stayed at the theater all day and into the evening performances. My father came to the theater. The ushers walked the aisles calling my name in hushed tones with their flashlights pointing to the floor searching for a nine-year old named Tony. Eventually, I was found and returned to my dad. The walk home was long and very quiet.

In my mind, life was good. We had things to do, places to go, people who cared about us, family get-togethers that were always pleasant, and two parents who wanted us to be happy, healthy, responsible, intelligent, and kind.

Our world was the neighborhood, the family, the church, the school, and the Yankees. How good is that?

Our town was the home of Tex the Cowboy who would draw on all the kids he saw walking with their parents. We also claimed bragging rights to the Peanut Man. Yep, while Tex kept law and order on one side of Main Street, the Peanut Man with his hard shell, spats, and high top hat would bow and pass out fresh-roasted Planters Peanuts to every kid he met on the other side of Main Street.

Rocky Castellani was a local hero. A boxer with a glass jaw who never gave up, he fought Bobo Olson for the middleweight championship of the world in 1954. Like the Rocky of the 1970s, he lost, but he captivated the imagination of every twelve-year boy in our town. One of my prized possessions was an autographed picture of Rocky Castellani. It was displayed in my bedroom for years.

Our values were deeply rooted in family, loyalty, hospitality, responsibility, and a sense of reciprocity. We were a "random acts of kindness" family long before the foundation that bears that name and mission was created.

My first experience with doctors came when I was in grade school. Along with my brother, sister, and a cousin or two, I was taken to Mercy Hospital in South Wilkes-Barre to have my tonsils and adenoids removed. It was not a pleasant experience. If truth be told, it was a very frightening experience.

I did not like the sounds, the sights, the smells, and the prospect of what was about to happen to me.

Since I was the youngest, my gurney was the last in line outside the operating room. The closer it got to the door, the more anxious I felt. Then it happened. I saw my chance, and I bolted.

What a scene! In the sedate Mercy Hospital, a little ink spot of a thing was running down the hallway as fast as he could with two or three adults in pursuit, one of them being my mother. She was embarrassed. I was scared. It was a recipe for disaster.

Eventually I was cornered, caught, and returned to my gurney. Dr. John L. Dorris, the biggest and most serious man I had ever seen to that point, separated me from my tonsils, and life went on with one caveat. I promised myself that day that I would never be a patient again. I kept that promise for sixty years.

Some fears last a lifetime.

During those two generations, my companions were fast food, stress, ambition, hard work, and periodic bouts with anxiety and depression. A worrier by nature, and a perfectionist by orientation, anxiety was a constant, uninvited guest in my world.

This destructive combination of friends came neatly packaged with a ribbon of a lack of confidence and insecurity. I masked these negative feelings with an air of self-confidence, indifference, and at times, insensitivity.

Whatever success I experienced in life resulted from a willingness to work longer, harder, and more intensely than most people so that I could achieve things that would honor my parents. That's where I found happiness and a feeling of self worth.

There was one unwritten but overarching law in our house. We were expected to do our very best. We were expected to make something of ourselves and in so doing bring respect to our family name. To this day, that expectation is a driving force in my life. I think Ken, Mary Claire, and I always wanted to make our parents proud in this way.

One of my very best days was the day I took my parents to Schaeffer Hall at the University of Iowa to show them the results of some of my examinations. I was unaware at the time that my father had fewer than two months to live.

When we left the building, my father looked at me and said, "I never made it out of grade school, but between you and your brother, I feel I got a college degree." It was my proudest moment.

Two other often heard aphorisms, "Whether the job be big or small, do it well or not at all" and "Once a job is first begun, never leave it until it's done," I learned from a handyman named Johnny Ferko whom I worked with in the Pocono Mountains in the early 1960s. These sayings, combined with one of my mother's proverbs, "Make hay while the sun shines," are central to everything I believe about work.

A combination of high energy levels and dogged determination, fueled by these blue-collar values and a willingness to delay gratification, enabled me to become the first Ph.D. and the first college professor in our family. My father did not live to see this day. My mother did, and I know it gave her great joy.

For me, it was not about being first; it was always about being the best that I could be. It was always about learning how to get better and how to become a better person. It was always about doing what others would not do. It was always about seeing defeat or failure as an opportunity to learn. It was always about picking yourself up, dusting yourself off, and starting all over again. It was always about being grateful for opportunities my parents did not have.

Somewhere, at some time, I learned that most Americans are excellent short distance runners, and, in fact, I was an excellent short distance runner. But in my heart and soul, I wanted to be more substantial. I wanted to be a marathoner. I didn't achieve that goal until I was sixty-five and close to death with four blocked arteries.

All those years before, I was a professional student and a caring person who admired people of compassion and courage. My heroes from childhood to adulthood were people who did the right thing even if they lost everything in the process. Case in point, my favorite movie is *To Kill A Mockingbird*. When I was in college, my favorite book was *Profiles in Courage*, my favorite social activist was Dr. Martin Luther King, and my favorite public servant was Robert F. Kennedy.

If you are wondering where I am going with this, the answer is simple. For most of my life, I was a man in conflict. I wanted the American Dream. I wanted to be popular, I wanted to be liked, and I wanted to do well. I wanted to honor my parents' expectations. I worked hard to get a good education so that I could have a good life, a good job, and the perfect American family. I soon discovered, however, that a life driven by achievement does not guarantee a life without disappointment and failure.

Along the way, there were bumps in the road: a heartbreaking divorce in 1977, two failed political campaigns that taught me something about ethnic animosity and bigotry, and a long period of soul-searching. A year of reinvention and transition in 1980 led me to a passion for documentary filmmaking and a new life dedicated to telling stories about ordinary people who give inspirational service to their communities and to their country.

It was a thirty-year period of all work, little play, great anxiety, high levels of stress, a fast food diet, high cholesterol, and denying the warning signs of heart disease that paved the way to Operating Room 5 at the Wilkes-Barre General Hospital and quadruple by-pass surgery that saved my life.

My heart scene journey of discovery and recovery was not without challenges. It was, however, a journey with far more opportunities to learn, grow and become whole than I ever imagined it would be.

My mother was right: "Tell me who your company is, and I will tell you who you are." The people I met and befriended on this journey gave me a second chance at life. They fixed my damaged heart, they helped me to heal a broken heart, and they enabled me to develop a much more positive and productive outlook on life. They helped me to better define, understand, and accept who I am as a person, a husband, a producer, a father, and a friend.

For me, open-heart surgery was the greatest learning experience of my life, and I am convinced that it can have the same result for the 500,000 Americans who have this procedure every year. That's why I am willing to open my heart and let you step in to learn how heart disease and open-heart surgery became my new best friends.

*My mother and father,
Angelo and Jane Mussari,
on their wedding day*

Tony Mussari 1947, five years old

My brother Ken and my sister Mary Claire

A DEFINING MOMENT

"Tony, remember this—life is for the living."
Brendan Vaughan

May 28, 2007, was an absolutely beautiful day. It was one of those days when you are just happy to be alive. The sun was high in the heavens. The sky was a beautiful azure blue. It was hot, but not too humid. It was a perfect day for a parade.

When I left Windsor Park that morning, I was singing the words from a song I learned as a child, "I Love A Parade." Written in 1932, the ninety-two words of this song were known to virtually every student of my generation.

To be more specific, these words were known to anyone who sang in the Glee Club at King's College in 1960, and they spoke to every parade I had ever seen: marching feet, brass bands, cheering crowds, military uniforms, fire engines, and, best of all, the Dalmatian.

Oh, how I loved those dogs. Restless, playful, with a mind of their own, and a tradition of service to firemen, I willingly went to every parade just to see the Dalmatian. I always wanted a dog, but my mother was not an animal person. Dogs and cats were not allowed at 27 Columbus Avenue. Rumor had it that we once had a cocker spaniel named Topper, but he mysteriously ran away one winter night.

At the parade, I could fantasize about having a pet Dalmatian. When you are less than three feet tall, eventually the parade noise gets to you, but the wagging tail and the welcoming look of the black spotted dog is a memory that remains forever.

On this spring day, a friend of ours was about to have a special moment. Atty. Harold Rosenn and his wife, Sallyann, would ride in the lead car during the Kingston Memorial Day Parade. I wanted to record that moment for a segment of *Windsor Park Stories*.

Like his brother before him, Federal Judge Max Rosenn, Harold Rosenn is a very special man: a World War II veteran, community leader, philanthropist, and lawyer extraordinaire. He is a likable person with a great sense of humor and great people skills.

To be quite honest, Kitch and I just like being with him. Every occasion is an opportunity to learn, grow, and discover.

Memorial Day 2007 would be no different.

Thanks to our friends, Elaine and Mike Blessing, I got the details on the parade. Mike, a retired Kingston police officer, told me how to get from one place to another with plenty of time to set up my camera before the parade arrived.

At 9:30 a.m., I left Windsor Park like a platoon leader on a mission. I wanted this shoot to go well.

One thing would be different, however, I would be alone. Kitch was on another mission. She was determined to get the lower gardens in shape for the garden tour that was just about a month away.

So off I went, unaware of what was about to happen.

Shortly after I arrived at Kingston Corners, I found a parking place that would permit me to cover the start of the parade, and then get back to the van and drive to the midway point in the parade. There, I would be able to get shots that were central to the story.

With the directions firmly planted in one cell of my brain, I would be able to find my way to the Forty Fort Cemetery where a brief ceremony would honor the memory of those who gave their lives for America.

At about 10:15 a.m., I found the red Mustang convertible that would carry the grand marshal and his wife. As I approached the car, I saw Atty. Rosenn and Sallyann. We exchanged pleasantries.

I took some digital pictures, and then I walked across the street to record the Wyoming Valley West High School band during warm-up exercises.

No surprise here. I love marching bands. (Thank you, George Parks and the University of Massachusetts Minuteman Marching Band!)

After taking time to cheer on the student musicians, I walked across the street to talk to the driver of the red Mustang about riding along with the grand marshal. She had no objections.

I squeezed myself and two cameras into the bucket seat on the passenger's side. Kneeling in a position that enabled me to capture the Rosenns as they greeted well-wishers, I felt a strange sensation in my stomach and some lightheadedness.

Then it happened. A pain like I have never experienced started in my stomach, made its way like an erupting volcano into my chest cavity, and then moved into my left arm. I had intense pain in my gums. Sweat began streaming off my forehead. A strange, but noticeable, pain filled my chest cavity and then my left arm. I felt weak and uncomfortable, disoriented, and I knew that something was radically wrong.

The pain became more intense, and I struggled to remain upright. No one had to tell me what was happening.

Since December 1990, I had been expecting this moment, and here it was. Like my brother before me, I was having a coronary event. It came without warning, and it was unmistakable and unforgiving. It was a most frightening experience, one I will never forget.

Not wanting to alarm anyone or take away from the beauty of Harold's moment, I asked to be let out of the car when it reached Kingston Corners.

Then, I made my way to my van. Once there, I quickly opened the aspirin bottle that was in my camera bag, and I took a Bayer aspirin with water.

The pain in my chest was constant, and I whispered a prayer to my brother Ken: "Don't let me die here...not here. Not today. Not without Kitch. Help me to finish this work."

In that moment, I was alarmed, stunned, frightened, but determined. I rested for a few moments, and when the pain stabilized, I pulled myself together, took a deep breath, and I considered what the next step should be.

As I carefully drove to the next stop on my schedule, I chewed a second aspirin, and, although noticeable, the pain in my chest, throat, and arm seemed manageable.

I parked the car, said another prayer, and I started walking toward Wyoming Avenue. As I approached the avenue to take up my position on the street, I literally bumped into a wonderful young man, Rick Stefanides, and his daughter.

Rick is a newcomer in our lives. He is a person with a great heart, and a value system that is deeply rooted in service and kindness. The day I met him in Windsor Park, he was helping his friend, another treasure, Mark McGrane. From the moment we made eye contact, I knew that Rick was my kind of person.

On this day on Wyoming Avenue, Rick and I exchanged pleasantries. I made no mention about what had just happened. Then, Rick and his daughter walked away, disappearing into the crowd of people lining the street.

The pain in my chest was real, but something told me I was OK. I took my position on the street, and I recorded the video I needed. Then, I walked back to the van. As I walked, I had a conversation with myself: *Should I go to the hospital? Should I go home? Should I finish the shoot? How serious is this?*

I suspected that I was having a coronary event of some type, but I honestly believed that it was not life-threatening. The pain in my chest was receding, and my situation seemed to be OK.

Was that a rationalization? Maybe. Was it wishful thinking? Perhaps. Was this the message I needed at the moment to keep moving forward? Yes. Would I suggest this as strategy for others? No!

As I posed a dozen different questions during several moments of reflection and private conversation, I thought about the things that were important to me: Kitch, my children Elena and Tony, Jr., y grandchildren, my parents and my family, my friends, the students I taught, Windsor Park and the television series that preoccupied almost eleven years of my life, *Windsor Park Stories.*

No matter what the question, however, the answer was always the same: *Don't overreact, Don't alarm anyone, You can't reach Kitch. You can do this. Remember what you taught your students: "Follow your instincts, remain on task, find a solution."*

Oh yes, there was one other thing running through my brain. *If I die doing this work, I will die doing something that I love to do.*

While all this was going on in my brain, I refused to think worst-case scenarios.

I made it to the Forty Fort Cemetery, the last stop on my schedule, and the last possible place I wanted to be.

There, I met a former student who is now a wonderful and trusted colleague, Warren Ruda. Warren is a photographer for one of our local newspapers, *The Citizens' Voice.* We have a very special bond. I forced him out of his comfort zone when he was an undergraduate.

In 1982, I invited him to become a member of our production team for a video shoot in Williamsburg, Virginia. Warren had never been out of the Wyoming Valley, and this was quite a challenging experience for a shy and retiring undergraduate, especially the madcap ride from Colonial Williamsburg to Harrisburg.

(Oh, by the way, the documentary we were producing was about the insanity defense. There must be a connection in there someplace, then and now.)

While we waited for the parade to arrive, we talked about his college experience, his family, and his job. State Representative Phyllis Mundy came by, and she gave us a warm greeting.

Later, I would meet the parents of a former student. They were very pleasant and very affirming. Their welcoming comments made me feel good. For a moment, I forgot my troubles.

Then, I talked with some World War II vets whose stories put a lump in my throat. They were sitting in wheelchairs sharing war stories with one another. I could not take my eyes off them. On this day, they looked old, frail, and tired. Nevertheless, there was a compelling quality of dignity and honor recorded on their faces and reinforced by the medals and the military uniforms they wore. These were the men and women of the greatest generation, and this was their moment to remember all their friends and neighbors who gave their lives for America. My pain seemed insignificant compared to their sacrifice.

The parade arrived. The ceremony began. I took some shots, and before leaving the cemetery, I took a special shot for a family history I was producing for a dear friend, John O'Brien.

I left the cemetery, and I drove the blue-lined roads back to Windsor Park. I was reluctant to take the Crossvalley Expressway for fear of an accident. As I drove, I thought about everything that had happened. I was shaken and worried. I whispered a prayer of gratitude that I made it, and I was on my way home.

Once home, I had a long conversation with Kitch. We planned a strategy that did not include a trip to the emergency room. You may wonder why.

The answer is simple. Several years ago during another illness, I did just that. I went to the emergency room. The hospital was under renovation. We were told to go to a designated waiting room, and for what appeared to be an eternity, the only thing we saw was a parade of construction workers carrying tools, pipes, electrical conduit, and other materials.

Frustrated and unable to make contact with the physician who was substituting for our family doctor, we picked ourselves up, and we went home. Two days later, he called to find out what happened.

"We got lost in the emergency room," I told him. "I decided I wanted to die at home. What happened to you?" I asked.

I never got a response, just this rejoinder: "Well, you sound OK, so everything must be OK."

My mother had a similar experience. After an apparent stroke, I took her to the emergency room of the hospital where she worked as a nurse for many years. For hours, she laid on a gurney in the hallway before someone recognized her and got her medical attention.

These memories set my direction. If this were to be my last day, it would be in a place where my humanness would not be violated.

After resting in the afternoon, we drove to Plains, Pennsylvania, to have dinner with our dear friends the Zikors. It was a lovely evening. The food was delicious. The conversation was enjoyable, and we laughed a lot. Virginia, Shirley, Karlina and John are wonderful hosts. When we left, we were rejuvenated by the gift of their hospitality. We got home sometime after 9:30 p.m., and we ended the day with a hug and a kiss.

During the early morning hours, I had another episode that woke me out of a sound sleep. The pain was just like the earlier cardiac event. I knew I was in serious trouble.

Fortunately, the aspirin therapy worked again.

Was my strategy the right strategy for others? No. It was, however, the right strategy for me.

Early Tuesday morning, I called my doctor only to learn that he would not be available until Thursday. Then, I heard the magic words: "If you are having problems get yourself to the emergency room."

When we did meet, he was concerned, serious, probing, and proactive. I like him, and I trust his judgment. The moment I told him about the perspiration, he got up from his chair. Looking at me with the most serious look I have ever seen, he asked, "Who is your cardiologist?"

I replied, cautioning him that I had not seen him since 1991. He left the room.

After what seemed like an eternity, he returned with an authorization for a cardiac catheterization.

The record of his copious notes taken during previous visits was very clear, three years of very stressful life situations, high blood pressure, and high cholesterol had taken its toll. I was lucky to be alive.

He ruled out a stress test because of what might happen. Instead, he arranged for a cardiologist, Dr. Michael Rupp, to do a catheterization. He wrote a prescription for nitroglycerin, and he ordered me to be very careful.

At the end of this very long day sitting on the balcony overlooking The Garden of Life in Windsor Park, Kitch asked me a question: "How are you feeling? Are you worried...depressed?"

"No. I'm resigned," I said.

The conversation ended.

Kitch is a master at understanding the moment. The peaceful sound of the water cascading over the waterfall in The Garden of Life was what I needed at that moment. She obliged.

We would have conversations like this several times during the four days between my visit with Dr. Michael Fath and the cardiac catheterization. They were days of worry and fear. The nights were worse.

Memorial Day 2007 was a defining moment in my life. I came face-to-face with my mortality. Apparently the coronary event took place in one of the smaller vessels in my heart. It was an event that produced damage that is reversible. In that respect, I was more fortunate than my brother.

I learned that day how precarious life can be. I learned what it is like to be aware that we are living on borrowed time. I learned that some unpleasant experiences lie ahead. I learned that my life would be very different moving forward.

I learned how fortunate I was to have survived the coronary event, and I resolved that if given the opportunity to have a few more years with Kitch, my grandchildren, and the people who matter most to us, I would take Brendan Vaughan's advice and make sure that our lives are for "the living."

Atty. and Mrs Harold Rosenn in the Grand Marshal's car where I had my cardiac event

South Maple and West Market Streets, the scene of my cardiac event

One of the cars in the Kingston Memorial Day Parade

Recording video at the Forty Fort Cemetery on the day of my cardiac event

The Diagnosis Is Not Good

"I know who you are."
Dr. Michael Harostock

When I left Dr. Michael Fath's office, I had an authorization for a cardiac catheterization, a prescription for nitroglycerin, and a zillion questions about where it would be done, the doctor who would be doing it, what it would be like, and how painful it would be.

To be very honest, I was frightened, worried, and very shaken by what I might be facing.

In the darkness of this experience, I turned to two family friends, Sean and Tom McGrath. They helped Kitch and me see through the maze of the medical decisions we were facing.

In the seventies and eighties, Sean was at our home virtually every day. He and my son, Tony, were fast friends.

His older brother, Tom, was a favorite of my father. The first-born to his parents Flo and Tom McGrath, he knows the medical profession in special ways. For almost three decades, he and his company, McGrath Medical Associates, have been involved with the implantation of pacemakers and defibrillators.

If ever a person was born to be a medical doctor, it is Tom McGrath. When that did not happen, he did the next best thing. He formed a medical company, and thousands of people with heart disease have benefited from his compassion and competence. He is one of the pillars of our community.

When Sean and Tom were infants, I held these youngsters in my arms, I watched them grow up and become consummate professionals. Now, they were literally holding me up as I approached the most important decision of my life.

Tom knows the doctors. He knows the hospitals, and he was most kind to both Kitch and me.

I was apprehensive, and Tom was able to put everything into context for me. He put my mind at ease when he spoke these words: "Michael Rupp is the best interventionist in the valley." His recommendations and suggestions were absolutely accurate.

Kitch and I spent June 7, 2007, at the Wilkes-Barre General Hospital. It was quite an experience: thirteen hours of tests, consultations, and discoveries.

I come from a family of nurses, and I know the workings of a hospital from the nurses' point of view. On more than one occasion, I found myself saying to every nurse who paid me any attention, "Both my mother and my sister were nurses."

I guess I thought this would get me better care. As my mother would say, "Any port in a storm."

It's funny the things you say when you are apprehensive.

The cardiac catheterization was interesting, painless, and uneventful from my point of view. The lab was cold. The nurses were friendly, and one in particular was very impressive. She was meticulous in the way she prepared the room. I liked her attention to detail; one of the other male attendants did not. He belittled her, calling her "Little Miss Hyper-Clean."

I found that remark offensive, and I could not resist rejoining: "I would rather her be hyper-clean than not. I don't want to be wheeled out of this room with something I did not bring in with me."

The lab grew silent.

A very pleasant nurse attached metal leads to my legs and arms. They were connected to an electrocardiogram that recorded the electrical activity of my heart during the catheterization.

A pulse oximeter was connected to my index finger. It measured oxygen levels in my blood, and it monitored my pulse during the test.

I was asked to lie still during the test. One nurse encouraged me to look at the monitor. I remember what an old friend, Bob Alles, said to me after he had the test, "Tony, it's fascinating. You can see everything."

The preparation work continued, and eventually Dr. Rupp arrived to do what he does best. He made an incision in my groin, and he carefully inserted a catheter into the femoral artery. He guided it to my heart. Once there he put a special dye into the catheter, and he injected it into my heart so that he could examine and take pictures of the various arteries leading to and coming from my heart.

Essentially, the procedure is a very complex X-ray. In fact, I could see the X-ray machine above me as I lay flat on the table looking up at the ceiling.

The objective is simple. Dr. Rupp wanted to determine if any of the arteries had been narrowed or blocked by plaque, the by-product of fat, cholesterol, and calcium.

For about forty-five minutes, I watched everything in real time on a monitor to my left. It was fascinating, but relatively meaningless to me. As I lay there as still as a church mouse, I thought about my first time with an X-ray.

When I was a youngster, I loved to go to the Father and Son Shoe Store. What an experience! While my dad tried on shoes, I put my feet in a machine that enabled me to see the bones in my feet and toes. How neat was that? In my adventurous little mind, I knew nothing about X-rays or the potential danger of overexposure. I just wanted to see the bones in my toes wiggle in real time.

Just when I was in high gear, my mother would enter the store, grab me by the arm, and pull me off this magical device with a stern look and a scolding. She knew something about the danger it posed to her youngest child.

With the number of times I did that little vaudeville act, it's a wonder that my feet don't light up my room at night. Here in this cath lab sixty years later, my feet were freezing cold, and it was my heart that was the main attraction.

For some reason, it just wasn't as much fun.

To the trained eye, cardiac catheterization is a roadmap. It enabled Dr. Rupp to check my blood flow and blood pressure in the chambers of the heart. He was able to check the pumping action of the heart. In minutes, Dr. Rupp was able to determine whether or not I had coronary artery disease and the extent of the resulting arteriosclerosis.

When the procedure ended, he gave me the results, and then he left the lab to speak with Kitch. I was moved to a room somewhere in the hospital. As I left the lab, I made a special effort to thank the nurse who worked so hard to make sure everything was right.

The results of my catheterization were not good... four blocked arteries. The descending aorta was 95 percent blocked, and three other arteries had 70 percent blockage. I soon learned an artery that is 70 percent blocked is considered to be a blocked artery.

Grim news, indeed. It was not what we expected.

I had hoped to get much better news. Maybe I would need a stent and be released in a day. That was not meant to be.

To say I was frightened is an understatement. I was petrified and disappointed in ways that are impossible to explain.

Why, oh why, did I eat all those french fries? Why did I put myself in such stressful situations? Why didn't I follow Kitch's lead and become a vegetarian? Why didn't I pay more attention to my mother when she warned us that fat, starch, and carbohydrates are no good for you?

I could see her standing in our kitchen and hear her saying to my brother, "You're going to have a heart attack."

In my arrogant, irreverent, know-it-all teenage mind, I thought to myself: "That will never happen to me. I am too active, too athletic, too smart to have something like a heart attack."

Well, sixty years later I learned the lesson of my life. My body chemistry and lifestyle had other plans for me, and it did not include an all expense paid trip to Hawaii.

In moments of great fear, you think about the craziest things. This was a very scary moment, and my mind was moving faster than an elevator in free fall from the top of the Empire State Building.

When I finally got my arms around my fears and I started to think clearly, I realized that this was not a time to be thinking about yesterday. It was a time to be thinking about tomorrow.

I stopped playing the old movies of my childhood and my life in the theater of my mind, and I opened a new high definition view of what tomorrow might be like.

To my good fortune, the Chief of Cardiac Surgery, Dr. Michael Harostock, was available to explain my situation. He is an unimposing man in his fifties. His smile is infectious. His eyes are caring and welcoming. His manner is professional and very human.

I liked him immediately. He made me feel comfortable. I sensed his competence and compassion. I knew instinctively that he was the person I wanted to do the surgery. In this case, the first impression was a lasting, positive impression.

Our first conversation sealed the deal.

He walked into the room, and he extended his hand as he introduced himself. When I tried to get up to extend my hand and reply, he interrupted with these words:

> I know who you are. I was an undergraduate at King's College majoring in biology in the 1970s. I was on the golf team, and I got to know you by your reputation. You were a no-nonsense teacher. You expected a great deal from your students, some of whom I knew. You were very passionate about what you taught, and you were a very intense person. You had very high standards, and you loved what you taught.

He paused, and looking me right in the eyes, he followed with a sentence that I will remember until the day I die: "I am honored to meet you, and I want to thank you for being an outstanding teacher."

Never in a million years did I ever expect to hear anything like that. It was one of the most important moments of my life. My apprehensions dissolved into complete trust. Many of the demons that came from the disappointments life gives all of us began to dissolve in this affirming, kind, unforgettable moment.

I am sure that part of what he said was protocol, but he personalized it in a way that touched my heart and made me feel good.

He was available. Kitch was characteristically optimistic and determined. We would go forward with the operation.

She liked Dr. Harostock for an entirely different reason. It was something he said later in the conversation.

We were talking about options, and I was hoping for a painless alternative. It was not meant to be, and Dr. Harostock was quite emphatic about that.

"I can guarantee two things," he told us. "This is something that you cannot cure naturally. If you do not attend to this, you will have more complications, and you will eventually die. I can't tell you exactly when, but you will die. You can't fix this with natural remedies."

The other thing he said was powerful on another level, and it touched Kitch's heart in a special way: "If you are uncomfortable with me, I will facilitate this operation at any hospital of your choice, because you must have this operation to live."

In that moment, Michael Harostock, King's College, Georgetown University Medical School, and The Ohio State University, proved to us that he was a special person and a surgeon with great confidence. To him, the life of the patient was more important than a business transaction. He connected with us on a personal as well as a professional level. I was willing to trust my life to this man who would eventually hold my heart in his hands.

He encouraged me to remain in the hospital, so that I could have the operation as soon as possible. In truth, I think he knew how frightened I was, and he feared that if I left, I would never return.

I had other concerns both personal and professional, and so we negotiated. He would see to it that I could go home for a few days, and I gave him my word that I would return for the surgery on Tuesday, June 12, 2007, at 8 a.m.

As we shook hands, I thought to myself that bolting from the gurney would not be an option this time.

Sometime after 2 p.m., I started a regimen of tests that would give the doctors information they needed to know prior to my open-heart surgery:

- A carotid ultrasound test to check for hardening of the arteries, atherosclerosis. It is a painless test that tells the surgeon whether plaque has narrowed the carotid arteries causing a risk for stroke.
- A pulmonary functions test to measure how my lungs were functioning. It is a painless test that tells the surgeon how the lungs will function during surgery.
- An arterial blood gasses test to determine the chemistry of my blood, oxygen and carbon dioxide, and to assess the capacity of my lungs to function properly during the operation.
- A test to check for hepatitis.
- A chest X-ray to give the surgeon an image of where everything is.
- Routine blood work to make sure there would be no bleeding issues, and to check cholesterol, triglycerides, and renal function.

Surgeons want to be sure that they have a complete profile of the patient before the operation. In the profession, they refer to it as looking at everything before they risk anything.

At some time after 6 p.m., we left the hospital, and we headed home. As we made our way to Windsor Park, I saw a billboard for The Heart and Vascular Institute at the Wilkes-Barre General Hospital that read: 20 Years of Open-heart Surgery Success, Over 9,000 Cardiac Surgery Procedures. I was about to become one more on that long list.

When we got home, all I wanted to do was put my head down and close my eyes. It was an exhausting day. Nevertheless, there were calls to be made, and things to do. Since I was restricted, Kitch attended to the cats. Then she went out to The Garden of Life. From my window, I could hear her talking to the fish in the upper pond as she threw them their dinner.

When she returned, she was tethered to the telephone. It never stopped ringing.

After a brief nap, I opened my e-mail account, and I began to read some of the notes. My eyes welled with tears as the emotion of the day burst like a dam in a flood. As I read the notes, a pattern developed. Those who wrote sent stories of encouragement. They offered suggestions, and they made comments about things they had done for us that day. They also talked about the impact *Windsor Park Stories* had on their lives.

It was a beautiful and humbling moment. So many people told us that they cared about our situation, our life work, and us. It was overwhelming and too much to absorb.

Several of the writers were people who had been featured on *Windsor Park Stories*. They were people who had great suffering in their lives. They are the people who gave me hope during the most difficult moment of my life.

For the next few days, I thought about what I was about to experience. The doctors told us the recovery would be at least six to eight weeks; however, we would feel the consequences of the operation for up to a year. On the positive side, if I made it through the operation, I would be blessed with a heart that should be able to function normally for about twenty-five years.

Kitch decided to move forward with two major events we had planned for the summer: the Back Mountain Bloomers Garden Tour, June 30, and the annual Irish Teachers Festival on July 28. She believed it would be something to look forward to, and it would be an incentive to expedite my recovery. I hoped she was right.

Together we attended to a number of personal matters. We did the things that had to be done. We paid our bills, and we identified all of our important personal items including insurance policies, mortgage documents, retirement accounts, long-term and short-term debt.

We talked about what we would like to do with Windsor Park, and how it would be maintained if things did not turn out well. But mostly we talked positively about the opportunity to have a second chance at life.

We read to each other the notes, cards, and e-mail messages. We made special arrangements for the room where I would stay after the operation. We made contact with the people we loved, and we tried to plan for all of the contingencies we might encounter.

In our public moments, we laughed, and sometime we cried. In our private moments, we wrote love letters, exchanged special messages, and we cried.

Always we felt the power and healing of kind words and positive thoughts. It was one of the most beautiful experiences of our life.

It's stunning how your outlook changes when you think you might die.

These four days in June taught us what life is all about, and how fortunate we were to be blessed with good friends and family who cared about us. These special days taught us how blessed we were by our partnership. They gave us an opportunity to learn how to cope with our fears, and they gave us some time to learn once again the power of prayer.

We were apprehensive and concerned, but we looked to tomorrow with hope.

Words of two unknown authors lifted my spirits:

—*Hope is grief's best music.*

—*Hope sees the invisible, feels the intangible and achieves the impossible.*

Before the day ended, I reread an exchange of letters I had with Chivon MacMillan, a dear friend, and the person who first suggested the word hope for The Garden of Life. These letters were written two days before my cardiac event.

Dear Chivon, Doug and Adam:

April 06, 2007

"The great Easter truth is not that we are to live newly after death— that is not the great thing—but that... we are to, and may, live nobly now because we are to live forever."

—Phillips Brooks

For the past several days, I have been thinking, reading and dreaming about Easter. I wanted to write something beautiful to you as an expression of our gratitude for your kindness and friendship.

Every time I tried to put the words on paper I came up empty.

In my heart and mind, I knew what I wanted to say, but I could not find the words. I was distracted and unfocused. Some medical problems, and two gigantic bumps on the road of life preoccupied my thoughts.

As I worked on our Easter Special for Windsor Park Stories, I heard the beautiful words from four

of the five inspirational hymns that comprise this
episode. They are:

Love isn't just for a day.
>>—*All That I Have*, Gary Ault

I am God, who comforts you, who are you to be
>afraid.
Of flesh that fades, is made like the grass of the
>field, soon to wither.
>>—*Turn To Me*, John Foley

When I am down and oh, my soul's so weary,
When troubles come and my heart burdened be,
Then I am still and wait here in the silence until
>you come and sit awhile with me.
>>— *You Raise Me Up*, Brendan Graham,
>>>Rolf Loveland

Like a rose trampled on the ground,
You took the fall and thought of me above all,
>>—*Above All*, Paul Baloche, Lenny Lebanc

I tried to craft a letter from these words. Beautiful
as they are, the writer's block continued.

This morning, while reading a book that was
given to us after we worshiped with you, Doug, and
Adam at the Princeton Alliance Church on Palm Sunday, I came across four words: The Hope of Easter, and
a window in my heart and mind opened.

Easter is about resurrection, rebirth, renewal,
optimism, love and faith. At its core, it is all about
hope. It's beautifully simple and very complex. I can
understand the simple part because it comes from

the heart, I will leave the difficult part to others.

My world is a world of images that spring from what I can see, hear, and edit. Hope, Inspiration and Service are central to the work Kitch and I do for Windsor Park Stories, and the series is central to our life.

So on this Easter Sunday, Kitch and I will give you the gift of a beautiful concert we recorded on March 4, 2007, in the Church of St. Ignatius. We love this program because it speaks to the yearnings, dreams, beliefs and innocence we had when we were children.

It speaks about hope.

In our opinion, when we strip away all of the walls we have built up over a lifetime, this is who we really are…children in adult frames hoping to find peace, security, love, understanding, forgiveness, kindness and friendship.

On Palm Sunday we were with you at your church. It was the most welcoming church experience we have ever had.

It was an experience that was rooted in the sounds of inspirational music, the voices of children praising God, the well thought out words of a sermon about celebration, and a diverse community of worshipers who were joined together in their faith.

As we left the parking lot of the church, we saw a sign that summarized everything we experienced, everything we were feeling, and everything we would like to say to you on this Easter Sunday.

"Go out with joy and be led forth by peace." This is a message of hope.

May the blessings of Easter be with you forever and may you always know that our journey toward joy and peace is centered in your kindness, understanding and friendship with us.

Doug's father will be in our thoughts and prayers this weekend.

We love the MacMillans,

—**Tony & Kitch**

Tony:
May 26, 2007

I have had this in my inbox since you sent it – I've read it several times before, including right now. How amazing that you speak of "hope" and that is the word I sent you in my previous email for the garden of life, BEFORE I re-read this one. The core of my hope comes from Jesus Christ – He is the hope for my future, and I pray, for my son's future as well. The whole message of the Good News is hope – Jesus came to earth, died on the cross, rose again to live in heaven so we might have HOPE for now and eternity. What a beautiful thing.

God has so richly blessed you with a heart of compassion – and the ability to craft words to convey that. May you give Him whatever burden you are carrying right now – He is faithful.

We love Tony & Kitch!!!

Love,

—**Chivon**

Chivon:
May 27, 2007

What can I say?

Providence brought us together so that we can

have hope for our children, our country, and our world.

One of the greatest blessings we have is our friendship with you, Doug, and Adam.

Kitch and I are eternally grateful for that, and we treat it like a precious gift.

From our hearts to your hearts, we love you in the way Christ taught us to love people with our hearts, our minds, and our souls.

What is so beautiful is that we always feel your love for us. That keeps us moving forward.

—Tony & Kitch

On this night when I thought my future was in doubt, the child in my adult frame found hope. I found it in the quiet competence of a surgeon with a heart of gold. I found it in the gentle and gracious words of a friend whose God gave her hope and the desire to share it with others. I found it in the kind and supportive actions of Kitch.

My body was restless, my emotions were fearful, but amidst the turmoil, I felt a sense of peace, the inner peace and confidence that comes from hope.

A reunion with Sean and Tom McGrath in front of the Wilkes-Barre General Hospital

A cardiac catheterization in progress

This is the billboard I saw on the way home from my cardiac catheterization

Chivon, Adam and Doug MacMillan arriving in Shanksville in 2007

A Prescription for Hope:
a Garden, a Song, a Kiss, and a Visit

My hopes are not always realized, but I always hope.

Ovid

More than anything else an open-heart patient needs hope. I know that in very real ways. When you first hear the news that you have heart disease that will kill you, you are shaken to the core. It is a frightening prospect for the strongest people. It is a crushing blow to your ego, your psyche, and your morale.

You are in a state of shock and denial.

How can this be? It happens to other people, but not to me. There must be some mistake about this. It can't be true.

The "I don't want to deal with this" reaction eventually turns to "I can't deal with this." If you are to survive, the next lyric of this song must be "I will deal with this."

That cannot happen without hope.

The question is where do you find hope?

It's not on sale at Best Buy. It's not available at Sam's Club. I never saw it advertised as a blue-light special at K-Mart. AOL doesn't celebrate it on its splash page, and to the best of my knowledge, no one ever videoed it for You Tube or My Space.

It's the darnedest thing. Hope is something everybody needs and secretly wants. It's essential for survival. Nietzsche tells us: "He who does not hope to win has already lost." Aristotle called it, "a walking dream." Reinhold Niebuhr told us, "We are saved by hope."

In my case, I found hope in all the simple places, all the unexpected places, all the human places.

I found it in a garden that celebrates life. I found it in the lyric of a song composed for a group called Brighter Light. I found it in a kiss from my sister and a visit from my cousin. I found it in the goodness of my wife. I found it in the words of a poet.

For me, hope gives energy, life, and purpose.

The Garden of Life in Windsor Park was a dream that preoccupied most of my thoughts during the fall of 2006 and the winter of 2007. Having finished The Memorial Water Garden celebrating the heroes of Flight 93, I was sitting in what Esther Heymann renamed The Angel Garden and thinking about a conversation I had with Brendan Vaughan during his last visit with the Irish Teachers Program. Brendan always emphasized the importance of living life to the fullest. Listening to his voice in my soul, it struck me that what we needed to best honor the heroes of Flight 93 was a garden that celebrated life. They died to guarantee life, and they would want us to get the most out of life every day.

Like everything else we built in Windsor Park, I put my thinking cap on, talked with Kitch at great length, spent hours sitting and walking the space in the vicinity of the Angel Garden, and I began to dream and to visualize.

Every evening I would close the day looking out my window at Windsor Park and thinking about how this garden would take shape.

One evening Kitch and I watched a *Hallmark Hall of Fame* presentation entitled, "In the Valley of Light." During the program, the famous Professor Fuller commercial overwhelmed me. The story of a chance meeting between a retiring college professor and one of his former students evoked an emotional response of volcanic proportions.

I identified with Fuller, and I wanted to know who provided the concept for this commercial. A letter to Hallmark connected me with Barbara Loots, a senior writer at Hallmark. Her work as a senior writer and poet was showcased in a series of Hallmark cards entitled *Secrets of A Joyful Life.*

Barbara responded with a handwritten note on a Hallmark card from that series. The words and the images on that card spoke to life. Whenever I thought about the card, the word life flashed through my mind. It was like the rough draft of an article or a first edit of a program. I had the concept. This would be a garden that celebrates life. Now, I needed to find the images and the substance of the design. A visit to Philadelphia would help Kitch and me refine the concept for The Garden of Life.

In March 2007, Kitch and I made our way to the Philadelphia Flower Show. It was something we had been trying to schedule for years. This year we decided to make it happen.

We went there to produce segments for *Windsor Park Stories.* The theme of the show was "Legends of Ireland," and that made it very attractive for us. Once inside the exhibition hall, we saw many beautiful water features, and one that we liked a lot. It was a two-tiered water feature with a rambling waterfall. The backdrop for this peaceful place was an Irish cottage with a thatched roof. This scene spoke to many of the most pleasant memories we had of Ireland and our visit there with Brendan Vaughan.

Shortly after we returned home, we decided to replicate this water feature in our front yard. We would capitalize on the shrubbery in front of our house, a beautiful weeping cherry tree that was given to us by Jackie Ross and her teammates, Timothy Heath and Jason Forbes, from the senior class in 2001, two forty-year-old white birch trees, and nine white pine trees that would frame the garden.

The construction began in early May, and it was not without its challenges. The contour of the land, the desire to make it an outdoor set for *Windsor Park Stories*, the need to have the garden flow out of the shrubbery in front of the house, and frequent rain storms combined to make every day an interesting experience.

At the same time we were building the new garden, we were renovating the room and the balcony that overlooked the garden. There was construction everywhere, and the attendant confusion, anxiety, and disruption that comes with all construction projects was ever present.

All this was happening without an architectural plan. As with just about everything I do, I was dreaming it, and visualizing it in real time.

This is the only way I know, but it is a roadmap for stress at its highest levels. Unlike most homeowners who undertake projects of this nature, I wanted to be fully involved, and I wanted to video every phase of the project while the crew from Edward's Garden Center was building it. This was easier said than done.

Thousands of pounds of dirt were removed and replaced with tons of rock and stone. The heavy equipment had to be carefully maneuvered around the existing trees. The original plan was altered a few times before we arrived at an upper pond with a biofall that emptied into a larger pond by way of a rustic waterfall.

Before the project was finished, it occurred to me that we needed something that would speak to life in this garden. The wonderful people at the Chatham Sign Shop in Chatham, Massachusetts, designed a sign, but something else was needed. It came to life with the help and talent of a creative person, Michael Sackett, in Forestville, California.

One afternoon during the construction, I was sitting alone in the unfinished Garden of Life. I was dreaming about the significance of this space, and what life meant to me. I was beset by two demons, my early retirement from teaching and my persistent struggle to keep *Windsor Park Stories* on the air. As with most days since 2005, I could not think clearly, because these demons distracted my attention.

Then it happened. Looking toward The Angel Garden, I saw a bird flying with grace and beauty against the azure sky, and the word "freedom" flashed through my mind. The freedom of the bird and the freedom the passengers of Flight 93 had guaranteed for all of us became apparent in new and significant ways.

The word freedom became synonymous with life, and I decided in that moment to ask family, friends, and supporters of *Windsor Park Stories* to share with us words they thought spoke to life.

On May 18, ten days before my cardiac event, I wrote these words in an e-mail to a select list of friends and family. It was titled Please Help Us Find The Right Words:

> The thought behind this garden is very simple. All of us are surrounded every day with messages of death, violence, destruction, and suffering. We experience it in the media, on the Internet, in our families.
>
> If you are like us, there are times when the sights and sounds of violence, death, and destruction just wear you down. You worry about our future as a nation, as a people, as a world.
>
> Kitch and I wanted to build something that speaks to life, to peace, quiet, and to serenity. We want something in the garden that will speak to the beauty of nature and to the beauty of human potential.
>
> In one of the last conversations we had with our dear friend, Brendan Vaughan, he spoke these words: "Tony, life is for the living!" Those words and everything that Brendan's life symbolizes inspired us to build The Garden of Life.
>
> The design and construction was phase one. The landscaping was phase two. The design of the sign was phase three, and what I am about to explain is phase four.
>
> Throughout The Garden of Life, we want to place words that speak to life, and we are asking for your help.
>
> We write this note to ask you to give us a word that in your heart, mind, and experience speaks to

life. The words you think best represent life will be permanently placed in The Garden of Life.

There are a number of suggested ways we can do this. At the moment we are thinking about having them painted on small rocks that will be placed throughout the water garden. If you have an idea, please share it with us.

We will dedicate this new water garden on Friday, July 27, during the Irish Teachers Festival. We hope you will be able to share that evening with us.

You should also know that this note is being sent to Brendan's daughter so that she will be able to suggest a word in her father's behalf.

In the weeks ahead, we will be writing to you about other activities connected with Windsor Park and Windsor Park Stories.

For the moment, we ask you to help us celebrate life in a garden that is dedicated to life, peace, joy and happiness. Your help and your friendship give us life, and for that we are grateful.

Sincerely,

—Tony & Kitch

The response to this note was overwhelming, and the unique character of The Garden of Life was born.

Michael Sackett of Let's Rock Carved Stone signed on to the project, and she agreed to engrave the words on rocks that would be placed throughout the garden.

Today one hundred rocks grace The Garden of Life. They speak to everything we believe life is all about. Among our favorites are: Affirmation, Apology, Bashert, Children, Freedom, Friendship, Forgiveness, Gratitude, Hope, Kindness, Laughter, Love, Mercy, Opportunity, Redemption, Respect, Sentiment, Service, and Sparkle.

Someone once said the most creative ideas come from private moments of simple questions and humble prayers. That is how The Garden of Life came to be. Little did Kitch and I know then how important it would become after my open-heart surgery.

The Good Shepherd Lutheran Church is a beautiful building in one of Pennsylvania's treasured small towns, Berwick. Known for its nuclear power plant, high school football, potato chips, and ribbons, Berwick is the home of the Brighter Light Choral Ensemble.

For twenty years, this group of magical voices brought hope and joy to thousands of people who attended their concerts. Until I received an e-mail from the public relations director of Brighter Light, I didn't have a clue about their great gift.

In February 2007, Luann DeGrose sent me a note about the members of her choral group. In her mind, the fifteen members of Brighter Light would provide a good human interest story for *Windsor Park Stories*.

She was absolutely on target. It took me three months to reply, but when I did, I committed to the story.

I liked the idea of a small family of singers who were passionate about their music of hope and inspiration. I was drawn to the group by one sentence in Luann's letter:

> With all the troubles in the world today, I felt it would
> be rather a heartwarming experience to feature a
> group of people who not only enjoy singing together
> and ministering to the public with their songs and
> voices, but who are also exceptionally close friends.

Friendship and loyalty are two very important values in my world.

On June 2, two days after our visit with Dr. Michael Fath and five days before my cardiac catheterization, Kitch and I drove to Berwick to honor a commitment to a group of people we had never met, in a place where we had never been, for reasons that defied logic and sanity. If truth be told, it was one of the warmest evenings of the spring. Just outside of Berwick, we had to turn around and drive back to Dallas, because I forgot the batteries for my camera.

That is just one indication of the state of mind I was in at the time.

Kitch was not happy with this decision. She knew I was taking quite a risk. I understand that now, and I certainly would not advise anyone to imitate my behavior. It was reckless and an indication of my advanced state of denial.

I did not, could not, and would not accept the seriousness of the situation. I could not see my heart disease. I was feeling fine, or so I thought. This was a wonderful opportunity to connect and expand the *Windsor Park Stories* family. I had aspirin and nitroglycerin. Life was fine, or so I thought.

There is only one way to describe what was going on in my brain, confusion, fear, and anxiety masked by a reckless determination to live as if nothing serious were happening. It was a classic case of denial.

There are many ways to explain what happened that night in Berwick. Only two have merit. I was very lucky, and Providence was with me.

Because of my forgetfulness, we arrived late. The church was packed. It was hot, and I was very stressed, but fortunately things went rather smoothly.

The members of Brighter Light were welcoming. We became fast friends. I liked their music. It was very inspirational. I admired the dynamics of the group. Their friendship for one another was very obvious. Their joyfulness was infectious, and their performance was excellent.

One song resonated with me on a number of levels, and it became my mantra for the next several months.

Written by Mary Hoida with music composed by William Cutter, "The Music in My Life" lifted my spirits, and it left an indelible mark on my soul.

I played it over and over and over again in the period before I went into surgery. When I came home from the hospital, I kept a copy of the lyrics on the desk next to my computer.

The words and the music of Brighter Light's 20th Anniversary Song, "The Music In My Life," gave me hope:

It is the music that makes me whole.
It is the music that sets my soul free.
It is the music that lifts my spirit.
It is the music that lets me be me.

For without music my life has no rhythm.
Without music, it has no rhyme.
Without music, it has no balance.
It's just the passage of time.

I thank God for the gift of my music,
And the people who hold the key
To friendship, love and inspiration,
And the doors it has opened for me.

It is the music that makes me whole.
It is the music that sets my soul free.
It is the music that lifts my spirit.
It is the music that lets me be me.
It is the music that lets me be me.

When you are five years old, and your sister is seven, life gets complicated. When it's 1947 and you are being raised in a very traditional family with deep roots in the church and a feeling that neighbors are watching your every move, life is very complicated.

My sister loved to boss me around. She loved to play with dolls, and because I was younger and smaller, she often dressed me like a girl doll and paraded me around the house. One day I resisted, and my world changed forever.

It's not that I did not like my sister. I liked her very much, but I was a boy and baseball and getting dirty was a boy thing. Playing with dolls was not!

I remember one day in the schoolyard at St. Mary's someone pushed me, and I pushed back. A circle formed, and soon we were slugging it out. For a little guy who was a year younger than everyone in his class, I was doing pretty well. Then my sister appeared, and she took my glasses saying something like, "Mother will kill you if you break your glasses."

Guess what? Mother didn't get the chance. The bully who was pushing me around finished me off because, without my glasses, I couldn't see very well.

Then there was the piano thing. My sister played the piano, and she was always practicing. She made a lot of noise, and I didn't like the sound. My parents thought it was beautiful music. I didn't agree. Guess what? My opinion didn't count for very much, especially with my dad. Mary Claire was his favorite.

Life went on. We grew up and somewhat apart. In high school, Mary became a cheerleader. I warmed the bench for the second-string of the varsity basketball team. I was too small to be a starter and too persistent to give up on basketball, the only sport our school had.

Mary graduated in 1957, and she went to nurses' training school at Mercy Hospital. In my opinion, she was the most attractive nurse in her class. I don't think I ever told her that. Brothers in the fifties didn't say things like that. They're probably not like that today!

I went to college, then graduate school and then to Iowa, and our lives changed in many ways.

Mary had the perfect family. I had a broken family having the unenviable distinction of being the first in my family to be divorced. It left an indelible scar on my heart that lasts to this day.

Then, without warning my brother, Ken, died from a massive heart attack. He was fifty-three years old. It was a devastating loss.

Ken was my brother, my hero, my anchor, my best and most trusted friend. I idolized him, and he had a very special place in his heart for me. When I was with him, I felt safe.

Most of what I had done in my life to that point, I did to make him proud. We talked on the telephone frequently, and visited with each other every chance we got. We loved to talk about politics, and he loved to talk about Penn State University football. He was true blue.

We were a partnership, but not of equals. Ken was always a step out in front of everyone I knew in goodness, service, spirituality, and insight. The day Ken died, the world stood still for me, and in some respects, it never was the same again.

The glue that held us all together was my mom. I don't think she ever recovered from Ken's death. The saddest thing I ever had to do was tell my mother her son died. It was more awful than any words can ever record. A few years later my mom got sick and needed permanent care, and that led to a number of family complications.

It happens because love takes on many definitions, and possessiveness is an essential part of the love of an only daughter. My sister thought my mother should live in a facility close to her home in New Jersey. I thought differently. She prevailed. I felt alienated.

By 2007, my sister and I were pretty much estranged. As someone once told me, we are not the Waltons, and no one in America is like the Waltons either. Mistakes, misjudgments, hurt feelings, petty pride, ego and poor conflict resolution skills complicate life for everyone. Whatever genius said what we need is an "Army of the Kind" was absolutely right.

In June 2007, my Aunt Jean became the commandant of the "Army of the Kind," when she told my sister about my cardiac event and my desperate situation.

In less than twenty-four hours, the misunderstandings of a lifetime dissolved in the warm sunlight of compassion and good-will. A telephone call that I treasure and a visit from my sister and her husband followed.

For the better part of an afternoon, we talked about just about everything I needed to know going into open-heart surgery. My brother-in-law, Jack Doyle, had the surgery nine years earlier, and he was more than generous with his time.

He shared everything he experienced, and he helped me to better understand what I was about to experience.

We talked about everything from pain management to breathing exercises. Throughout it all, my sister was there to help Kitch better understand the operation from a caregiver's point of view. It was about as close to a Waltons' moment as we have ever had.

The hour was getting late, and it was time for Mary and Jack to return to New Jersey. Then it happened.

My sister rose from her chair. Without warning, she came over to my recliner, and she kissed me on the forehead. It was a kiss of love, affection, support, and peace. It was one of the most beautiful moments of my life. In my heart and mind, it washed away all of the misunderstanding and frustration that comes from sibling rivalry in a family of overachievers.

It was a family moment, a beautiful moment, a moment of strength, encouragement, and joy. It was a moment of goodness and great hope. We were united again as brother and sister. We came together in a caring and supportive way. We were what my mother and father always wanted, united and at peace with one another.

It's amazing what happens when two people let their hearts rule their actions in the name of peace and comfort. In the words of the lyricist, it was a moment when we let love in.

During my childhood, my cousin Kathy Pulaski and I were inseparable. For a time, I thought we were brother and sister living in separate houses. According to family folklore, whenever my mother needed a break from parenting, she sent us to visit Kathy's mother, my Aunt Sara, on Dana Street about three blocks from our home. As I remember, it's a walk that took us up the street and around the corner. In those days, everyone walked everywhere, and everyone in our neighborhood knew everybody.

We were located half a block from Rossi's junkyard as I called it, and about the same distance from the Salvation Army. In the other direction, there were two garages that housed trucks from Purvin Dairy. No one ever worried about walking anywhere. The sidewalks were always crowded with walkers.

Once we reached my Aunt Sara's house, it was like being in heaven. She was a happy, smiling member of a family that was serious by nature. Sara was different.

Like all good things, the good times ended when Kathy's dad moved the family to New York, and it wasn't until I was a freshman in college that we began to see one another again.

I loved the excitement of New York City, and Kathy's dad had connections so we got to go places and see things that were really special.

I remember as if it were yesterday our first visit backstage after a Broadway performance. In those days, I was smitten by Julie Andrews and her roles in *My Fair Lady* and *Camelot*. I never got to met her, but Uncle Ed saw to it that I met another Eliza Doolittle, Margot Moser, backstage at the Mark Hellinger Theater.

What a moment.

The plain fact of the matter was I enjoyed being with Kathy, and because of our friendship my world expanded beyond the confines of the Wyoming Valley. Life was good, and we enjoyed every minute of it.

Then we grew up and took on the responsibilities of marriage, raising a family, and all the things that preoccupy parenthood.

Despite all of the unexpected things life had in store for us, our friendship remained a constant.

Fast forward to June 2007. When Kathy O'Toole heard about my impending surgery, she got into her SUV and drove to Windsor Park from her home in Hopewell Junction, New York. It was a day of friendship at its best.

Together we laughed and cried as we shared stories from our past; the time my cousin Jimmy and I threw her in a Holiday Inn swimming pool not knowing that she could not swim. Yes, we saved her, and yes, I tried to sleep on the floor next to the couch where she was recuperating only to have her dad put me out of the house. My Uncle Ed was not a sentimental kind of guy when anyone put his daughter in danger.

On this day, a woman of great dignity and class, a woman of great faith, a woman of great perseverance, a woman who personified everything I admire in a human being drove to Windsor Park from upstate New York, just to be with me, to express her concern, to offer encouragement and support for both Kitch and me, to give me hope.

There we were, two people in their sixties, with all the road-rashes everyone earns during a life of parenting and caring. We were still standing. We were still friends, and according to Kathy, we would be standing together long after this current bump in the road was fixed.

On this day, my cousin came to hold my hand and tell me I would be all right. It was a beautiful moment, a family moment, and a memorable moment.

Ask me where I found hope, and I will tell you it was in the garden, in the music, in the kiss, in the connections with family and friends. It was in everything Kitch did and said from the moment she learned about the cardiac event. We had each other and a feeling that we were going to make it through the operation and beyond.

I found hope in the optimism of my wife, a woman who knew something about death and dying.

On Father's Day weekend 1961, Francis X. Loftus died of a heart attack. On that day his first-born child watched in stunned amazement, not knowing what to do or how to help. It was the most painful and defining moment of her life. Forty-five years later she was determined that the man in her life would survive, because she was filled with hope and resolved to do everything right.

When our house emptied of family and friends and the quiet of the night spoke to the fear of tomorrow, Kitch was there with love, kindness, support, and hope.

Kitch is the music in my life. She is hope.

In my mind, Emily Dickinson described Kitch when she wrote these lines:

"We'd never know how high we are till we are called to rise; and then, if we are true to plan, our statures touch the sky."

The Garden of Life in Windsor Park

The entrance to Windsor Park

Brighter Light in concert, June 2, 2007

The song that gave me hope

TODAY IS MY TOMORROW

While I thought I was learning how to live, I have been learning how to die.
Leonardo Da Vinci

June 11, 2007, was one of the most difficult days of my life. I was nervous, anxious, fearful, and very worried. For most of the day, I was beside myself. I couldn't and I didn't sleep. It was the day before surgery. My mind, heart, and emotions were pulling me in many different directions.

The memory of the visits of my sister and my cousin lifted my spirits. They gave me hope, but another side of me saw the possibility of death, and that was a very chastening reality.

I was frightened, and frightened people do desperate and unexplainable things. I was no different.

Early in the morning at about the time of the robins' first serenade, I got myself dressed, and I quietly left Windsor Park for a destination that held many memories from my childhood, St. Mary's Cemetery in Hanover Township, Pennsylvania.

I can remember my mother taking me there to visit the grave of my grandfather. I can remember painting the fence and cutting the grass in that cemetery, a job I held during the summer between my high school graduation and college.

This morning I felt compelled to go there to visit with and feel the presence of four people who had a profound influence on my life: my mother and father, Agnes O'Brien and Sister Mary Hilary.

I am sure psychiatrists would have a field day interpreting the meaning of this decision. For me, it was both reasonable and comforting. These were four of my heroes. People who helped shape my life. People I admire, respect, and feel obligated to please. People who taught me the meaning of almost every important value I know. If truth be told, only one person was missing from this pantheon of heroes, my brother Ken. His final resting place is in a cemetery in Sykesville, Maryland.

When I arrived, the cemetery was closed so I parked on the street, and I slipped under a chain that barricades the entrance.

First I visited the grave of my parents. It's a simple, blue-collar-solid memorial designed by my mother in 1967. Ironically, it is located in a place that was an empty field of grass in 1959. Every week I cut that grass with a gasoline-operated walking lawn mower, all those years ago when I needed to earn money for college.

The stone bearing our family name was covered with early morning dew. The rising sun covered the grave with gentle rays of light. Standing there in silence, I thought to myself how fortunate I was to have been born to these two people who sacrificed everything for my brother, my sister, and me. A thousand images from my years at 27 Columbus Avenue and 289 East South Street flashed through my mind.

I could see my mother in her print dress with her hands on her hips, her facial muscles tight with anger and fear as she yelled at the top of her voice, "You're going to school." It was the summer of 1947. I darted into the street without looking, heading for my favorite cherry tree in Jerry Schmidt's yard on the other side of the street, unaware of a Purvin Dairy truck that came to an abrupt stop to avoid hitting me. The physics of the moment was simple and catastrophic. Cases of fresh milk went crashing through the back door of the truck spilling bottles all over Columbus Avenue. It was not a pleasant moment.

Monsignor Francis Costello saw to it that my schooling at the parish school would start one year before my time. In some ways, I have been paying for that reckless dash all my life.

It is one of the reasons I visit the cemetery, and every time, before I leave, I whisper words of thanks that the truck and my mother did not kill me. On this morning, the ritual changed. After I thanked my mother and father, I asked them to help me find the strength and the courage to face whatever tomorrow would bring.

As I walked away, I turned to look back at the grave of my parents. One more time I whispered the word *thanks*, and wiping the tears from my eyes, I walked to a section of the cemetery I first visited in 1958.

I met Agnes O'Brien when I was a freshman in high school. Her goodness, gentleness, and kindness made an indelible mark on my heart, and to this day, she defines most of the things I admire in a woman. She was smart, witty, and oh, so welcoming. She always made me feel at ease, and she always went out of her way to include me in the group of students who palled around with her oldest daughter, my classmate, Patricia.

The O'Briens had a summer cottage at Harveys Lake, and many a day Agnes would pull up in front of our home on East South Street and pick me up so that I could join the other kids in her car and spend the day at the lake. Her green Pontiac station wagon has a special place in my memory, and her thoughtfulness taught me a powerful lesson that I have never forgotten: Be kind and inclusive.

Agnes O'Brien died in childbirth when I was a junior in high school. It was a sad day for everyone in my class. For most of us, it was our first encounter with death in a personal way. As a tribute to this beautiful person, I arranged the honor guard of students who lined the steps outside of Holy Savior Church in East End and at the cemetery in Hanover Township.

On this June morning, I came alone to this place to ask Agnes to help me. Ask me why? I can't give you a reasonable answer. It was something I had to do, I wanted to do, I needed to do. Working on the McDonnell family video with her son, John, I saw her picture again and again during the editing sessions. It helped me recall her warm and caring ways. It reminded me of a special time in my life and the important role she played. Somehow, I knew that she would help me, and I needed all the help I could get.

The greatest thing a parent can do for a child is to give him the desire to learn. The greatest thing a teacher can do for a student is to help him maximize the opportunity to learn.

Sister Mary Hilary, R.S.M., was the most important teacher in my life. Without her there, my life would have turned out much differently.

When we met, I was class president, and so full of myself, I could not see the perilous road I was traveling. My world was preoccupied with rock 'n' roll music, jitterbugging at the Catholic Youth Center with my good friend, Ellen Doyle, listening to Elvis Presley, and rushing home after school to watch Arlene Sullivan, Ken Rossi, Justine Carrelli and Bob Clayton dance on *American Bandstand*.

Our world was simple and uncluttered. We had nothing of any material value. We didn't yearn for very much, and we were happy in our little world.

On a personal level, life was good. I was popular, and the Yankees were winning. In the 1950s, popularity was the ultimate measure of success!

Sister Hilary changed all of that. She did what all good teachers do. She forced me out of my comfort zone. She made me come to terms with my potential not on the dance floor or the baseball field, but in the classroom and in my soul.

One day when I was embarrassingly unprepared for class, Hilary took me aside, and with these words she changed my life: "Mussari, from now on when I assign six pages, you will do ten." I thought she was being unfair. Before I could get the words I was thinking out of my mouth, she taught me another lesson I needed to learn: "And if your don't like it, and you think you're such a tough guy, go out to the coat room and punch the radiator."

That was vintage Hilary, all five feet one inch of her. That was the most important class of my lifetime. That is what I needed to hear, not what I wanted to hear, and that is what helped me to become a man.

Sister Hilary and I became fast friends on that day. It was a friendship that lasted a lifetime, and it continues in a spiritual way as I write these words. She was my mentor, my teacher, and my friend. She helped me paint a portrait of what I could be, and I have been refining that painting for more than forty years.

On this day in June, I needed to be with her. I needed to talk to her, I needed to feel her presence in my terrified and torment-ed soul. I needed her strength, spirituality, and wisdom. I needed the comfort of her caring and compassionate ways. I needed the prayers of this saintly woman who memorized all of the Psalms, and knew and taught the beautiful message of Mystici Corpus Christi, the Mystical Body of Christ on Earth.

On this day, the theology Hilary taught us had special meaning. I was looking for Christ in every person I would meet tomorrow, and I was hoping they would find a small part of Him in me.

So to the flat ground marker that records her life in a plot re-served for the Religious Sisters of Mercy, I went. Once there I asked my teacher to help me, to pray for me, to guide me, and to give me a second chance at life so that I could live it in a quality way, doing what she taught me to do, giving service and hospitality to others.

In so many ways, it was the most selfish thing I did that morn-ing. I was begging for my life in a place that honors the dead. Yet, it was the most human thing I did on that day. When I left, I felt stronger and more prepared for what I was about to face.

Kitch spent a good deal of the day getting ready for what was about to happen. She spent a good part of the afternoon shop-ping for things we would need. She recorded her activities in her calendar diary with a red magic marker: shoemaker, Wegman's, Bed Bath and Beyond, East Mountain Inn, reservations for The Irish Teachers Festival. There were no embellishments.

For most of the afternoon, I was alone with my thoughts and fears, and I did what I had been doing since the bad news arrived. I sat at a makeshift desk in my room overlooking The Garden of Life composing a letter from my heart to my close friends and family.

Entitled *Waiting for Tomorrow*, it was an attempt to express everything I was feeling, fearing, hoping, and praying:

> For most of my life, I have been waiting for tomorrow hoping it would be better than today, praying that somehow I would be wiser than yesterday, wishing that the mistakes I made would be forgiven, thinking that hard work and self denial would be affirmed, believing that most people are fair, just, decent, and kind, wanting to be like everyone else, but knowing that just was not so, dreaming big dreams for the students I taught, the children God gave me and the people who worked in the offices next door, yearning for opportunities that would enable me to help and serve, praying for a world that would know peace, searching for answers to questions that most people don't ask, believing that goodness is its own reward, and always teaching that the road to leadership and self-fulfillment came through the parking lots of: affirmation, service, enthusiasm, flexibility, and loyalty.
>
> These things I learned from the men and women of the Greatest Generation. I know no other way.
>
> Today, tomorrow is here for me. Soon my heart will be in someone else's hands. It's an awesome, beautiful, frightening feeling.
>
> As I approach the most defining moment in my life, I am strengthened by the good tidings of hundreds of people who have written words of encouragement and hope.

In these precious moments, I write to affirm the beautiful thoughts that will give me strength, hope, trust, and the ability to dream.

What follows here are a few of the words that will make my tomorrow possible. They come from the good hearts of people who care about what really matters in life. They care about human things, nature's things, God's things.

I share them, because I feel compelled to give them away so that when you face your tomorrow, they will give you hope.

For years, Kitch and I tried to teach a very simple philosophy that we first learned from an inspirational speaker with a name no one could pronounce, Lautzenhauser. It went like this:

You can't lead others until you lead yourself.

You're only worth what you give away.

You can only give away what you have.

For us, these were more than words on a page; they were commands of the heart and soul.

For most of my life, I have practiced these words with reckless abandon, always trying…always caring…never giving up and always dreaming of the best that could be in me and others.

If my tomorrow turns out well, you can be sure that Kitch and I will resume our journey knowing that we owe our very best to everyone who took the time to help us during this difficult time in the shadow of tomorrow.

If my tomorrow ends today, I know in this wounded heart that I always gave my very best, and I never gave up.

I have had five loves in my life: my family, my children, Kitch, King's College, and my twins, Windsor

Park and *Windsor Park Stories*. Virtually all of the good tomorrows came from these loves. I approach my defining moment knowing I gave each of them the very best that I had. Always thinking of them first and always dreaming the dreams for them that never were but could be.

I can hear a train whistle blowing in the wind and the water cascading over the waterfall in The Garden of Life outside my window. These sounds remind me of childhood fantasies and adult accomplishments both made possible by my parents whose faces I can see in the night and whose voices tell me that I have been a lucky man indeed.

As I make my way to the cold room with the bright lights and skillful hands that will hold my heart, these are some of the caring words you wrote that will give me strength to face my tomorrow.

I thank you for your kindness and your caring hearts,

—**Tony**

Dear Tony and Kitch,

Would you let me know what day the surgery is so I can mark it on my calendar and keep you both in my prayers. It's hard enough going through the surgery, but having sat and waited for my mother to come out after triple by-pass, its also very hard for those waiting.

She also had a main artery blocked and had suffered the mild heart attack first. This happened about a year before you met her and as you could see, she looks great and is so glad to have gotten a second chance. I spent the first week home with her and it was hard, but better than not having the second chance. All my best to you both,

—**Janet Allen Hall**
Luzerne County Convention and Visitors Bureau

Tony

Know that our prayers and thoughts are with you here at Misericordia. I will be entering your name on the Prayer List. I hope someone will keep us posted of your condition. I personally will be thinking and praying for a complete recovery.

God Bless You, Tony and all the trained personnel who will be attending to your medical needs.

Fondly,

—**Judy Ellis**
Misericordia University

Tony,

Our thoughts and prayers will be with you tomorrow. If it's any consolation, Brighter Light would be honored to sing at your Irish Teacher's Festival and Garden dedication on July 27...we have agreed to be there and are looking forward to the road trip and spread our love for music and ministry.

You need to continue telling your stories. God has a plan for you and this is it. This must go on, so there's no way you're leaving.

Good luck and God Bless
—**Luann DeGrose, Brighter Light**

Hi Tony:

I remembered you at Mass and lit a candle for your complete recovery. I think you have a book in the making which, in a way, you already started. Thanks also for the kind and generous words from you and Kitch. We wish you well. Be good to yourself as you have been to so many people and your students.

Thinking about you,

—**Bill Gaydos**

Doc,

It was very upsetting to me when you were telling us the story of that Memorial Day and the Parade. I thought to myself, this can't be happening. It brought me right back to when my grandfather was sick and the same thoughts and emotions all came back. You are such an important person in my life and I guess I didn't realize something like that can happen to all of us.

Love,

—**Karlina Zikor**

Kitch:

Please either call me or write me an email to let me know the results. My family and I will keep you in our prayers. Doc, I know you love doing what you do...but please take it easy. Please?

Love,

—**Tiesha Brunson**
North Hollywood, CA

Doc,

I heard you are having-open-heart surgery.

I hope everything is going well and there are no complications. It's a scary time, but I'm sure you're in good hands. I'll keep you in my thoughts and prayers.

Take care,

—**Phil Yacuboski**

Dear Tony,

As I was reading every word of your message, I got to the part where you said sweat starting pouring, you felt weak and was having some pain. I knew immediately what was wrong as I went thru the same thing. Again, I waited, because I was at work at Blue Cross as a Manager. I felt I could not leave my post. By the time I got to the hospital, my heart stopped 3 times. I was lucky. They sent me to Robert Packer Hospital for emergency surgery. I am so glad that nothing happened to you for waiting. We will be thinking of you and saying a prayer for both you and Kitch.

With All our Love,

—**Jan, Kerrilee, Molly**

Called aside —

From the glad working of your busy life,
From the world's ceaseless stir of care and strife,
Into the shade and stillness by your Heavenly Guide
For a brief time you have been called aside.
FOR ONLY A BRIEF TIME

—**Jan Ginley**
Connamara Dancers

Dear Tony— Please know that you are in the thoughts and prayers of many. We wish you God's Speed through your surgery and recovery.

Love,

—Your Cousin , Diane Dreier

Dear Doc,

I can't believe it! I know you must be getting tons of emails/letters/cards but wanted to write as soon as I read the email a minute ago. I am so sorry to hear this. However for my part in the encouragement dept, I have to tell you an uncle of mine had a very similar diagnosis a few years ago and underwent surgery as well. It took 2-3 months for him to recover but recover he did and the main thing is, he has his life back and better than ever. He had major cholesterol issues as well which lead to the blocked arteries so he really watches what he eats now too. I think it was a wake up call for him that said he had a lot more living to do as do you. You have a lot left to tell the world through Windsor Park Stories and your experiences. I myself wouldn't be the person I am today without your help and guidance back in the early 90's at King's...ok I'm dating both of us but you get the gist :) Please know Jeff & I will be praying for you and that the outcome will be great. I know you, you are a fighter so hang in there and we will be thinking of you in the next weeks to come. If you can have visitors after the sur- gery/when you are up to it, we would love to visit.

Take care and know you are loved,

—Jen Davis

Tony & Kitch

Absolutely nothing in our lives is preordained or predestined.

Only God can do that and he is all-powerful and utterly and completely benevolent. There is no human reason and certainly no metaphysical reason why you cannot continue your meaningful, important work

—John Lucas
Penn State University

Dear Tony and Kitch,

To say I'm speechless, is a definite understatement! You remind me of my father who drove himself to Nesbitt Hospital while in the middle of a heart attack....then called my mother from his bed and told her she might want to come over before it was too late and he wanted to see her again..."one more time." He did survive and live to be 85 years old.

You and Kitch have been in my heart ever since we met. You see, You and Kitch are the unsung heroes of Windsor Park Stories, more so than those you identify and capture on film or in word. without you both, people like myself would never have balance in their lives....that's what Windsor Park does for me, it provides the balance that I have looked for so long.

To remain so positive in the midst of so much chaos and fear....I believe that your faith took over and you listened to what God told you to do....questionable sense...but thank God for you, it worked.

Many years ago, I was on disability...over seven years...there were times that I'd felt I was never going to come out of it..times when I really didn't want to

come out of it if I were to have to live with the prog-
nosis with Lupus that usually occurs. For the first time
in my life, I felt vulnerable. Again, faith played a role...

Faith and love are all one really needs to enjoy
living this life God has given us...it all boils down to
faith and love of family and friends. Apparently God
still wants you to remain here for your family...you
passed the faith test.

God bless you and I want you to know that I
have St. Luke on the job...working for you so that all
remains well for you both...I prayed to St Luke for
myself (and look how well I'm doing) and all those I
care about who experience health challenges...so..I've
pulled out the big gun now. He has a direct line to
Mary and the Big Guy!

Let us know how everything turns out and....if
there is anything I can do for you both...don't hesitate
to call on me...and that's not an idle offer. I mean it.

—Ruth Kemmerer
Director, Resource Development & Volunteer Services
Family Service Association of Wyoming Valley

Dear Tony,

What a total shock this is....I am praying that your call
from the cardiologist was a good one. I am calling the
Home of the Good Shepherd, with a prayer request
for you. They are Contemplative nuns who pray ALL
DAY and they have a very good track record.

I am praying for you and will await the GOOD
NEWS!

Love,

—Patti Brooks
St. Paul, Minnesota

HI TONY-

YOU KNOW... I READ YOUR NOTE.... AND KNEW BY
THE TITLE. WHAT WAS COMING.

ANYTHING I CAN DO? I'M SURE YOU HAVE A
GREAT CARDIAC PHYSICIAN.. BUT IF YOU'RE UNHAP-
PY IN ANY WAY.....LET ME KNOW. I HAVE ACCESS TO A
VERY GOOD ONE.

WON'T CALL. BUT YOU CAN ANYTIME. I'M HERE..
TO SUPPORT YOU BOTH... IN ANY WAY I CAN.

LV-

—MIKE LEWIS

Dear Tony,

You opened my heart when I needed it. Now, your
heart is going to open even more tomorrow...the love
from all of us will be with you.

May God bless you and Kitch tomorrow. I will be
praying continuously throughout the day for you. You
are loved and cherished by many.

You have touched many lives. I thank God for
meeting you. I look forward to the day we meet
again. Like Herb Brooks, you're a fighter, a dreamer
and a believer. Believe now.. God Bless You.

Love,

—Julie Marvel
Moraga, CA

Tony,

You are in my prayers. I am going to go over to St.
Mary's and light a candle for you there. (So many
good memories there. I just had a flash back the

other day of the Saturday morning phone calls from your mother asking if Michael and I could come down and serve a wedding that afternoon. She was always so good to Michael and I with scheduling us for the "paid" services! LOL She was great and I know she will be watching over you tomorrow. Can you believe I can still remember your wedding at St. Mary's with Msgr. Madden and then the party in the backyard on Grant Street, afterwards. Tony and I had so much fun the next day smashing what was left of the Ice Sculpture before you guys left for Wildwood, NJ - the honeymoon at the VIP! I think I was left on Nike duty that week and you gave me Salt Water Taffy from Douglas Fudge and $20 for my services - I felt like a rich man that week!)

Hey buddy! You get well. I'll respect your privacy and not bother you until I hear from you. Please let Kitch know to call me if she needs anything at all.

I love you buddy! Everything is going to be OK. God Bless!

—**Sean McGrath**

Tony,

I was very sorry to read about your health problems. My wife Nancy and I will keep you in our prayers that I can promise. Stay strong in mind and spirit as best you can. Also remember, now you will feel guilt free when you use the handicap parking space at the PO (just kidding)

—**Jim (The Postmaster) Mc Andrew**

Tony,

God speed Pal. Your news took us by surprise with a feeling of shock and unfairness. But rest easy my friend, you will be fine with a brand new set of pipes. Catching it now is certainly God's blessing upon you. You have many more miles to go. Be assured you are on my mind and in my prayers.

—**Kevin Blaum**

Dear Tony and Kitch,

Bless you both. I know that all the normal--and even those beyond normal--support systems will be sustaining you both as you go through the surgical experience and the recuperative process afterwards. You are in good hands and the outcome will be positive.

I wanted to touch base so that we acknowledge to each other the impossibility of your being in Hyde Park for the Freedom Court dedication events on Friday. I am truly sorry that you will miss what is shaping up to be a rather moving ceremony.

Know that Jane and I will be thinking of you and praying for a successful surgery and recovery.

Much love,

—**Chris Breiseth**
Hyde Park, NY

Hello Good Doctor...

Mom, Dad, and I send our prayers to you. Things will work out for you.

As I reach for comforting words, all I can think of are the words you taught me, which I find myself using daily. I'm doing well, and carry you with me in everything I do. The Show of Shows 10 years ago seems like just yesterday. The day after, I ran my season-ending bowling tournament, and kept my word, thanking each and every bowler. I did the same thing yesterday. It felt good, and I know all the kids appreciated it.

You were a big help to me in my formative years. I hope my kind words are a comfort to you.

Best of luck and good fortune.

Love,

—**Travis Sparks**

Dear Tony:

Pat Kirk has written of your upcoming heart surgery. Know that you are lifted and loved from this house-hold and by Jim and me.

We pray God's wisdom for those who will minister to you through fixing the heart to wholeness and for your body as it continues to serve you monumentally.

She also writes and plans to send photos of the waterfalls you have created and the memorializing of the victims of the PA Flight 93 plane crash. I marvel at your capacity to bring about angels and memories and honor. Thank you.

Blessings now to you and Kitch as you face a surgical time in your life, seeking long quality of life.

God says "I am able." 2 Cor. P.8, and so it is.

Peace, hope and love,

—**Pastor Dee Donnelly**
Atlanta, Georgia

Tony & Kitch

As I read your e-mail this am I bowed my head and prayed that God would watch over you and bring you good results. Your mark on this troubled world is needed and it must go on. You bring beauty to us all. I'll be waiting to hear the results.

May God give you peace over the outcome.
Love you both and think about you everyday.
Love,

—Janie Kiehl
Shanksville, PA

Dear Kitch

I have a special mass tomorrow for Saint Anthony of Padua and I will certainly be praying that Tony has a complete and smooth recovery. Keep me informed and let us know the address of the hospital and room.

Vince, Geri, Jason, and I are all very concerned. Thanks for the update.

—Bill Gaydos

Hi Tony,

We just wanted to send along our best wishes to you for a successful surgery and speedy recovery.

Our thoughts and prayers are with both you and Kitch. Could you please tell us when your surgery is scheduled? I will pass it on to Msgr. Hrynuck and he will pray for you specially on that day.

You are so used to being on the go all the time that the hardest part for you might be that you have to take it easy and slow down for a while.

Just take it one day at a time and time will be your ally. Before you know it, you will feel like a new man. God Bless.

—**Roger & Beverly Barren**

Dear Doc & Kitch,

I just got back into town today after some quality family-time in Chicago. I found your email waiting for me today.

About 2 years ago my father had his first heart attack while at home. He was shocked several times before being whisked away to the hospital. The diagnosis was a clogged artery.

Cutting to the chase: Two tremendous things happened as a result of that day: (1) My father quit smoking after 30 years of 2-packs a day. He is alive and very healthy now with a new lifestyle. And (2), my sister decided to pursue a career in nursing after seeing the work they do first-hand.

Someone once told me that hospitals are awful places, but what would we do without them. I know that some good and something new will come out of your experiences.

Take good care...

—**Alan Brocavich**

Dear Tony and Kitch,

Be assured of my special prayers at this difficult time.

I trust that all will go well and that you'll be better than ever after the quadruple-by-pass surgery takes place. My thoughts and prayers are with you.

—**Sr. Mariam,**
Marywood University

Doc,

Best of luck to you tomorrow.

Please know that we will be praying for you. In no time you will be feeling much better. We love you.

Love and God Bless,

—John, Virginia, Karlina, and Shirley Hahn

Dear Mr. Mussari:

Thank you for your msg on your progress. I know in my heart everything will be fine. You have a lot more things to do, We need you.

My prayers will be with you.

A new friend,

—Bev from Old Forge

My God, Doc!

I am so sorry I have not responded to your e-mails sooner, but I have been so crazy that I did not open them until yesterday.

Please, please, please know that you are in my heart and my prayers. I will say an extra one for you tonight. Just remember that you are a man with a lot to offer and a lot to look forward to.

I love you, Doc.

Wishing You The Best,

—Jerome Maida

DEAR TONY AND KITCH.

I JUST FINISHED READING YOUR EMAIL, I WANT YOU TO KNOW THAT MY PRAYERS ARE WITH YOU

AND I KNOW EVERYTHING WILL BE OK!!   PLEASE,
PLEASE CALL OR EMAIL ME, I KNOW I CAN HELP, ANY
HOUR, ANY DAY.

I WILL TALK TO YOU OVER THE WEEKEND FOR
SURE, PLEASE LET ME HELP YOU THROUGH THIS. IT'S
WHAT I DO!

ALL MY LOVE

—ELAINE Blessing

Dear Tony:

I am deeply touched by your story. I remembered you
at Mass tonight.

May God bless you and the doctors and may you
have faith in them, and yourself, The God who created you guides you and loves you.

Take good care,

—Fr. Tom O'Hara, C.S.C.
King's College

Tony:

While your life has been amazing and full, and you
have touched people all over the world while impact-
ing lives everywhere, (including mine), your dash is
not complete!

To see true wealth one needs only to look at you.
You are rich beyond means, with a wife, family and
friends who love you, (including an adoptive grandson
in NJ), the gifts that you "give away" through Windsor
Park Stories, your home and grounds, and most importantly your true love and friendship for others.

You have weathered the storms of life with class
and dignity. You continue to see the silver lining in

the midst of storm clouds while setting the bar higher for you and those around you.

You have never settled for less, instead you always reach for the true potential. Your potential still awaits you.

Your gifts have not all been given away yet. Many lives still await the crossroad meeting of the Mussaris.

So get healthy, try to relax and distress, but more importantly keep working on your dash! As always you are in our prayers, thoughts and hearts.

—Doug MacMillan
East Windsor, NJ

Sometime during the morning, the first shipment of rocks for The Garden of Life arrived. Could it be that Providence made it happen that way? The way I was thinking it was as probable an explanation as any. At that moment, what mattered most was the beauty and the workmanship. It was Michael Sackett at her very best. The different shapes, colors, and sizes were just what we wanted.

Looking at the words that would grace this special space, I forgot what I was facing, and with the enthusiasm of a child on Christmas morning, I went to The Garden of Life. My eyes canvassed every inch of the water feature, and I found a prominent place for the word "service." I picked this word because it is central to everything that is important to Kitch and me.

Quiet, well-intentioned, altruistic service to others may not make headlines, but it gives me hope and happiness. It makes life worthwhile.

I'm sure Sister Hilary was smiling.

Mussari family tombstone

St. Mary's Cemetery

*Words of Life
in The Garden
of Life*

*My teachers: Sister Felician, my brother Ken, his wife, Shirley,
and Sister Hilary*

The Sound of Silence

Silence is the mother of truth.
Benjamin Disraeli

If the day before my surgery was difficult, the night was even worse. I didn't want to eat. I didn't want to talk. I didn't want to sleep. It was the most unusual feeling. I just wanted to be alone with my thoughts.

As the immortal Seneca said, this was "a season for silence."

For what seemed like an eternity, I sat in my room or stood on the balcony overlooking The Garden of Life thinking about my wife, my family, my children, and my life. I thought about what had been, what might be, what I feared, what I wanted, and what I hoped could be.

As images from my life flashed through my mind, I slipped deeper and deeper into a reflective, melancholy mood.

As much as I wanted to concentrate, I could not concentrate. I thought about Kitch, Tony Jr., and Elena. I thought about some of the students I taught. I thought about my parents and my brother and sister. I thought about our beloved Rose, Kitch's mom. I thought about a few close friends who never wavered in their friendship. I thought about dreams dreamed, dreams fulfilled, and dreams that never materialized.

I thought about the future of *Windsor Park Stories*.

I thought about days of marriage, graduation, births, and deaths. I recalled classroom scenes, location shooting scenes, and scenes from a special moment in 1968 when the world seemed upside down, and we looked to Bobby Kennedy to bring us a newer world.

I thought about a lot of things, but mostly the times I didn't measure up, the times I stumbled, and the times I was human and made mistakes. It's been that way for most of my life. I rarely think of accomplishments. I always think of the need for improvement.

On this night, I thought about what death would be like. Where would it take me? Who would I meet? How harsh would the judgment be? Those questions came straight from my traditional Catholic upbringing. In the forties and fifties, God was a jurist not a benevolent father; the emphasis was on accountability not forgiveness, justice not love. Once that image of God becomes a part of your being, it is almost impossible to get it out of your mind.

Growing up Catholic made an indelible mark on the first twenty-four years of my life. Everything my family did was in some way tied to the church. We knew no other way. Our home was devoutly Catholic. Our school was Catholic. Sunday was Catholic. We went to Mass not the mall. We said grace before and after meals. We prayed the family rosary, because we believed what Father Patrick Peyton Said: "The family that prays together stays together." We always prayed for the souls of the faithful departed, and we never ended a day without evening prayers.

Some of us prayed the Angelus, a beautiful devotion traditionally recited three times a day in churches and convents. The name of the prayer comes from the opening words Angelus Domini Nuntiavit Mariæ:

> The Angel of the Lord declared unto Mary.
> And she conceived of the Holy Spirit.
> Behold the handmaid of the Lord.
> Be it done unto me according to thy word.

And the Word was made Flesh.
And dwelt among us.
Pray for us, O holy Mother of God.
That we may be made worthy of the promises of
Christ.
LET US PRAY

To this day, the Angelus is my favorite prayer, thought of frequently, said rarely, but never forgotten.

During my childhood, the dream of every mother was to have one of her children become a priest or a nun. If truth be told, that was the first aspiration of my brother, and one that I entertained as a member of St. Anthony's Vocation Club. Believe it or not, I still have the bright colored lapel pin that told the world I was thinking about a vocation.

When Fr. Peyton came to town, thousands of people carried their rosaries to Artillery Park in Kingston, Pennsylvania, and every Catholic school student, myself included, stood in formation to pray the rosary in public.

In my day, boys were taught to respect girls. Girls like my sister were encouraged to be Mary-like in their dress and behavior. The images of Fatima and Lourdes were central to our thinking, and the goal of every day was to do those things which would enable us to be good so that one day we would have life after death in heaven. There was a big emphasis on death and judgment.

On Saturday evening, we lined up to go to confession. At my church, there were four wooden confessionals in the basement of the church. We lined up on either side of these three chamber structures. The priest sat in the middle chamber, and two penitents knelt on either side. You always knew when it was your turn, because the priest would slide open a wooden window, lean his ear to the screen, and softly say the sign of the cross in Latin. The penitent would respond with these words: "Bless me father for I have sinned." Then he would list all of his sins including the number of times the sin was committed.

Somehow the boys always knew which confessional housed the kindest and most understanding priest, the one who did not raise his voice, or give you a long penance.

When we were young, we got the impression that good was defined by counting how many times you did not do this or that. It was a defensive, self-absorbed kind of goodness that made you feel like you were a member of some exclusive club, not a member of a community of the kind. We were Catholics, and we were taught in word and in action that somehow we were better than those who were not.

The Catholic Church was the most influential force in our lives. We did not question. We obeyed. We served. We supported, and we loved our church. It was, in our minds, what the church fathers taught us: "It was the one, true, Catholic, and apostolic church," and Christ was our redeemer. We would meet Him and his mother on the last day.

The church of my childhood was a beautiful place of worship. To this day, I can see in my mind's eye the huge painting of the crucifixion framed in gold carefully positioned above the main altar between four Roman columns, the stained glass windows, and the ornate marble altar. On Sunday, there always was a solemn high mass with a robust choir singing Latin verses, while a small army of altar servers made up of boys like my brother and me served three priests dressed in golden vestments who were held in high regard.

There were ceremonial rituals for every season, and a set of rules for every occasion. Church membership made life simple and very uncomplicated. Everything was good or bad, black or white, right or wrong. Nothing was gray.

The Baltimore Catechism helped us learn which was which. We memorized the rules, and we marched down the aisle of life in perfect single-file, lines that made our parents proud.

Our parents, the nuns, and the parish priests taught us well. We were true believers.

On this evening, all my early years of Catholic education came to the surface, and I thought about the times I didn't measure up, the times I strayed from the truth as the church taught it, the times I questioned, and the times I doubted. The times I didn't or wouldn't walk single-file down the aisle of life.

In recent years, I lost weekly contact with the church of my family. The church that I loved as a child and the teachings that were so important to me as a young adult still have profound meaning, but the structure and administration of the church, the legalism of the church, the authoritarianism of the church, the commercialism of the church, and the insensitivity, and smugness of certain representatives of the church made it a place where Kitch and I did not feel welcome.

I saw myself as a Catholic in belief, someone who was struggling with the road rashes of life, someone who yearned for a connection with the church of my father and mother when a conservative pastor whom we had never met and who knew virtually nothing about us, our life situation, our spiritual needs or our charitable undertakings sent Kitch and me an officious form letter telling us we were being placed on an inactive list at our parish church. The letter told us the decision was made because we had not been to church in a long time, and we had not made contributions to the church in a long time.

If there is anything I have learned about the setbacks life gives all of us, it is this. In times of crisis, we need people who have the gift of reconciliation. None of us should be punished by decisions without discussion. In moments of conflict, misunderstanding, and alienation we need people who are blessed with the spirit of compassion, caring, conversation, sensitivity, and social justice. Our world needs people who know how to heal the wounds that come with life and make people feel that they are valued and belong.

In an increasingly impersonal world, we need the gift of humanness. We need the kindness of an understanding heart.

I learned this from a master. It happened in 1959 in front of St, Mary's High School on South Washington Street. I was seventeen years old, and, by any standard, I was having a very bad day with my high school principal.

To my good fortune, I met Father Andrew J. McGowan, a young priest who was the spiritual director of our high school, as I was leaving the school building. My head was down, my posture slumped, I was embarrassed and hurting. He sensed something was wrong, and in his caring way, he listened while I explained what happened as only a teenager can with urgency and hyperbole. He looked at me, and he saw beyond the obvious.

On that day, in front of that grand old school building, he said and did something that changed my life. Putting his hand in his coat pocket, he took out some change, and he said, "Tony, here's some money. Go to the movies. I'll take care of the problem inside. Everything will be OK."

I went to the Paramount Theater on Father McGowan's dime, while he worked his magic with my principal. It was one of the most beautiful and lasting teaching moments of my life. He taught me in action what he would explain to me later in life, his belief in the priest as reconciler.

Almost half a century later, the memory of that moment and the impact of that lesson are as vivid as they were that day. It was a cornerstone moment in my life. I experienced and never forgot the kindness of his understanding heart.

On this day in June, I was looking for the priest as reconciler.

In more than two generations of church membership, respect for the clergy, and love for the church, I experienced in real and personal ways the agony and ecstasy of my church: the harsh corporal punishment of some of our teachers, the anxiety-filled and frightening moments of the confessional, the spiritually paralyzing horror of sexual abuse, and the arbitrary and capricious behavior of some clerics and church leaders.

At the same time, my generation was blessed by the words of Bishop Fulton J. Sheen, the leadership and legacy of Pope John

XXIII, the thoughtfulness of Cardinal Joseph Bernardin of Chicago, the beautiful and inspirational stories of Father Joseph Girzone and Sister Dorothy Ederer, and the kindness and compassion of a saint named Mother Theresa. These are the people who defined the church that inspired me. These are the people who helped people like me heal the wounds of life.

The goodness and decency of several Religious Sisters of Mercy from Misericordia University and two members of the Immaculate Heart of Mary order from Marywood University helped Kitch and me maintain a connection with the church of our parents

There are many other people who do the work of the church in beautiful ways connecting rather than alienating people from their God's place of worship. One such person is a young Holy Cross priest, Father Patrick Hannon, the author of *Running in the Arms of God*. Father Hannon's God is a God of love, a God who teaches that the power of love is always greater than the love of power.

On this night of reflection, fear, and worry, I yearned to be connected to a spiritual force. I wish I had been connected rather than alienated from my church. I felt like I was caught in the pull of two powerful magnetic forces: the God of love and mercy and the God of righteousness and judgment. I prayed to the God of love for his forgiveness. I feared the wrath of the God of righteousness.

In the end, I accepted my humanity. I stepped out of the shadow of fear believing that I did my best and knowing that the rest was in His hands. I knew in my heart of hearts that I would be accountable for everything I did and everything I failed to do. I took comfort in a prayer and a quotation ascribed to Mother Theresa:

> People are often unreasonable, illogical and self-centered;
> Forgive them anyway.
> If you are kind, people may accuse you of selfish, ulterior motives;

Be kind anyway.
If you are a success, you will win some false
     friends and true enemies;
Be kind anyway.
If you are honest and frank, people may chide
     you;
Be honest and frank anyway.
What you spend years building, someone could
     destroy overnight;
Build anyway.
If you find serenity and happiness, people may be
     jealous;
Be happy anyway.
The good you do today, people will often forget
     tomorrow;
Be good anyway.
Give the world the best you have, and it may
     never be enough;
Give the world the best you have anyway.
You see, in the final analysis, it's between you
     and God anyway.

In the darkness of great anxiety, my tormented soul was look-ing for God, the God this saintly woman said could not be found in noise and restlessness. In her words: "God is the friend of si-lence...we need silence to touch souls."

Another matter that weighed heavily on my mind was the future of *Windsor Park Stories*. For most people, this is a locally-produced television show. For Kitch and me, it is a way of life. For more than a decade, we sacrificed everything to build the outdoor set for the program, Windsor Park, and to develop and grow the series and keep it on the air.

Windsor Park Stories was a staple of our local public televi-sion station for years. Our audience was not large, but we had a loyal family of viewers who found our 7 p.m. time slot on Sunday evening to be convenient and an alternative to commercial programming. For more than a decade, we provided a kind of television that is difficult to find these days.

One viewer called *Windsor Park Stories* "television for the soul." Another wrote: "Imagine how nice the world would be if all of our stories were *Windsor Park Stories.*" A former student called the series "Chicken Soup for the American Soul," and then he wrote this: "The premise is simple—beautiful stories being told in beautiful gardens by even more beautiful people." Others told us they liked the positive messages. We designed it to be television about non-celebrities who had stories of hope, inspiration, and service.

It is a fun show to produce, because it connects us with real people and it provides an opportunity for us to help people. Our viewers like what they see. Their feedback provides the incentive we need to they keep moving forward. We love the people we meet, the stories they tell, the places we visit, and the things we learn producing the series.

It takes us from our perennial garden, Windsor Park, a serene and peaceful place crafted out of a community dump to places like Cape May, New Jersey; West Point, New York; the Library of Congress in Washington, D.C.; Lower Broadway in Nashville, Tennessee; the home of coach Herb Brooks in St. Paul, Minnesota, to name but a few.

After the horror of September 11, 2001, Windsor Park Stories took us to Ground Zero and Point Thank You in New York, and Shanksville in western Pennsylvania. Our *What Is America?* series began in the ashes of the World Trade Center, and it continues to this day as we produce at least one story about September 11 and the heroes of that day every year.

We organize a visit and screening in Shanksville every year. We consider Shanksville to be our second home. We have made a determined effort to keep the memory of Shanksville alive, and we carry the spirit of Shanksville with us every day of our life. It is as close as The Angel Garden that celebrates the heroes of Flight

93 just steps from our front door.

Wherever we go we meet and interview the kind of people who don't get an opportunity to tell their stories on commercial television. We love the challenge and the opportunity *Windsor Park Stories* gives us.

In January 2006, the music of *Windsor Park Stories* abruptly stopped. A conflict over artistic freedom, the hurt feelings that result when two friends discover the emptiness of what they thought was a lifetime friendship, the demand that we submit our programs for prescreening, and our career at public television ended.

We were without a home, but what we believed in remained intact. It was an awful time. It was a stressful time. It was a very lonesome time. It came six months after my retirement. It came just at the time we were experiencing major family health issues. It came almost without warning, and it was just one more thing that contributed to my own health issues.

Recently I discovered that my stress levels between 2004 and 2007 were constantly in the 80 percent range. During that time, I was skating on very thin ice. Virtually everything that gave me a sense of purpose was changing, and I was having great difficulty adjusting.

My strategy was to work longer and harder. It was a surefire recipe for a variety of problems.

To our surprise and good fortune, we had an agreement to be back on the air in three months. Our new life in commercial television began after a luncheon with a friend in our home and a meeting with the general manager at the local NBC affiliate, WBRE TV, John Dittmeier.

We liked Dittmeier from the first hello, and we got the impression he liked us and our work. He was an open person. He told us WBRE TV was honored to have the show, and there were ways they could take care of the cost of the time. He recognized that it was a labor of love, and we were motivated by community service, not huge financial reward.

We were very optimistic about our future at WBRE TV.

If truth be told, in the years *Windsor Park Stories* has been on the air, we have always been able to cover our expenses, but there has never been anything left over for salaries or any other financial gain. That never deterred us from pursuing our dream. We always saw the community service aspect of the series as an important motivation for producing *Windsor Park Stories*.

As fate would have it, fewer than two months after we settled into our new television home, the general manager who was so kind to us was dismissed. For the next several months, we were in a state of uncertainty.

During this time, we worked harder than we have ever worked. We changed the format of the show. We produced segments virtually all over the state including a priceless two-part series with Amish photographer, Bill Coleman, in an Amish village he called home for 35 years.

We wanted to earn our place in commercial television. We wanted to capitalize on this opportunity to produce the best local television program possible. We wanted to become part of the family in our new home. We wanted to make Windsor Park the most peaceful and attractive outdoor set in Northeastern Pennsylvania, a place where people would feel comfortable telling their stories.

It was our dream, a dream that was intimately connected to the transition we were experiencing from a career in teaching to a retirement of serving our community with *Windsor Park Stories*.

In a very real way, we were implementing what Vincent Van Gogh said about his work: "I dream my painting, and then I paint my dream."

Toward this end, we constructed and financed what today is called The Angel Garden, a water garden decorated with the forty Angels of Freedom and designed to celebrate the heroism of the passengers of Flight 93. It is a beautiful space. It was dedicated on July 27, 2006, and appropriately named "The Angel Garden" by Esther Heymann, the stepmother of twenty-seven-year-old Honor Elizabeth Wainio, one of the passengers of Flight 93. The following year we built The Garden of Life and a microgarden we call The Children's Water Garden.

For six months, we worked tirelessly to prove the merits of *Windsor Park Stories*. We traveled from Philadelphia to University Park, from Choconut Township in Susquehanna County to Williamsport in Lycoming County recording scenes for segments about our favorite places in Pennsylvania. We wrote seventeen articles for the Windsor Park Theater; we agreed to participate in the area's largest garden tour. We covered a fascinating conference about grandparents raising their children's children and the Luzerne Foundation's annual meeting hoping to make some contacts for our Windsor Park family. We organized the largest summer festival we had ever sponsored. We agreed to produce an hour-long historical documentary about the family of a friend, John O'Brien, and we scheduled our fifth annual visit and screening in Shanksville, Pennsylvania.

It was a period of intense activity, stress, mounting debt, and work unlike any other in the history of *Windsor Park Stories*.

On the day before my surgery, we were told in a telephone conversation that the station wanted the show, but we would have to pay for the time. It was the last thing I expected to hear on that day, at that time. It was the last thing I wanted to be thinking about on the day before my surgery. I was looking for hope, and I got a good dose of reality.

It weighed heavily on my mind during recovery. It tested everything I taught my students about life and being a professional in a world of commodification. It was the instrumental cause of one of the most important lessons I learned about life during my heart scene journey: disappointment is the mother of opportunity.

It reminded me of a poem Carl Mays wrote for his book, *Winning Thoughts*:

Stay

It's easy to give up
When the going is rough.
It's easy to hang your head.

But to carry the load
When the others won't,
That's the challenge instead.

As you fight against hope
and your chances are slim,
it would be easy to crawl away.

But hold your head high.
It's not time to die.
Now is the time to STAY!

I was disappointed, but determined that if my surgery were successful, somehow, someway, Kitch and I would keep *Windsor Park Stories* on the air.

As I drifted further and further into deep thought, the telephone rang. When Kitch brought me the telephone with a broad smile on her face, I listened to the voices of my daughter, Elena, and her husband, Jeff. They called to lift my spirits. They had positive words, encouraging words, helpful words. They made me laugh. For a few minutes, I forgot about all the things that troubled me and everything else that complicated this evening. The soothing words they spoke about my grandchildren, and all that we would enjoy after the operation and the recovery was a gift of healing. These were words of life that I needed to hear.

After the telephone call, Kitch and I talked about Elena and Tony, Jr. It was like so many conversations we had had over the years. Elena is my oldest child. She is a resourceful, problem-solving, independent person. She is a natural conversationalist who enjoys people. She is a talented graphic artist who teaches at a community college. She is a sensitive human being who loves her children, but she and her husband, Jeff, have high standards for them.

Elena's world is a world of animals, books, gardens, libraries, and the Washington Capitals hockey team.

When she was a child, people would say to me, "Elena is ten going on thirty." She was always older and more responsible than most children. Like all children of divorce there is scar tissue, but she has never used it as an excuse or let it get in the way of her dreams.

About the only time I worried about Elena was during her senior year at Bowling Green University. One night she called to tell me her apartment was being watched around the clock by the police, because a boy whom she knew told her: "If I cannot have you no one will have you. I know where you live, I know where your parents live."

It was a scary time, but Elena handled it with courage, good sense, and determination. Fortunately, the episode was resolved by the university without incident. Elena graduated, and on that day, she pasted a word to her mortar board that spoke volumes: RELIEF.

Fast forward about six years. It is a beautiful spring day. My daughter and son-in-law are standing in my seminar room teaching my students in a way that would fill any father's heart with joy. It was one of the very best days of my teaching career.

Tony Jr. in my son. He is a very intelligent, a very athletic, and a very likable person. When he was a child, his summers were preoccupied with Little League baseball and the Philadelphia Phillies. As he grew older, soccer, baseball, and football preoccupied his time.

In high school, he was a talented soccer player who was encouraged to try out for the football team by his biology teacher.

One day he walked onto the practice field and asked for a tryout. He made the team as a kicker, and for the rest of his junior year he saw limited game time.

During his senior year, he was the value-added his team needed to win its first championship in thirty-plus years. It was a Cinderella story that did not have a Cinderella ending. With Kitch and two wonderful students, Katy Finn and Amy Fixl, I recorded this championship season in a documentary called *Friday Night Heroes*.

Early in the last and championship game, Tony was hurt by an illegal tackle after he kicked an extra point. It was a deliberate foul. He was carried off the field. He returned to kick off, and even the commentator remarked about his resilience. In the last quarter of the game, Tony missed a short field goal and then a very long attempt of almost 50 yards. His team lost, and in my opinion, his life changed forever.

He went to college, but he was never the same. Something happened inside of my son, and it paved the way to a life of risks that did him and his parents no good. His battle with depression, alcohol, and gambling created moments of exasperation, frustration, anxiety, and worry for everyone who loved him.

Again and again I tried to intervene, but it all fell apart during a Christmas visit in 2004. Things never have been the same between the two of us since the day I put my foot down and said enough is enough. Advised by professionals not to empower him, not to pull his irons out of the fire, not to affirm his destructive coping mechanisms, I followed their advice with the tough love they suggested.

I have never had a peaceful day since, but I am convinced I did the right thing.

On this night, I had thoughts of appreciation and gratitude for Elena and thoughts of worry and concern for my son who had successfully completed a rehabilitation program. I wondered if he knew what was about to happen. I wondered if he would call.

I wondered if he would care. It was another night of agonizing about decisions I made and worry about this boy whom, like his sister, I love more than life.

Someone once said when something is wrong with a child, there is no happiness in a parent's life. Like far too many parents in America today, I was working too hard and too long in pursuit of the American Dream. At the same time, I was searching, hoping, and praying for a solution for the problems my son faced. It is the worst feeling to watch your child suffer. It is even worse when a child disowns you, because you refuse to be a part of his self-destruction.

At one point in the evening, I thought to myself, if I don't make it, maybe one of his problems will be solved.

The hour was getting late, and I decided to turn to one of the things that gave me peace of mind. I opened my e-mail account and I began to read some of the messages that filled my mailbox.

Scrolling down the list I saw Tony's name. I quickly opened the note. His three sentences touched my heart. They gave me hope.

> Dad,
>   I hope everything goes as planned. I'm not sure of all the details but I will be thinking of you and praying for you. If I can do anything, please just let me know.
>   Love, Tony

My response was quick and from the heart:

> Thanks Tony:
>   This will be my most defining moment. Four blocked arteries. Major surgery, and a long and inconvenient recovery period. If I make it, they say I could have 25 more years. If I don't, well, for the most part it's been a very good ride, as my brother once said.

> For you and me the road in the past several
> years has had its twists and turns, but one thing is
> absolutely certain: I love you today in the same way I
> loved you when you were born.
>   That is a constant that never changed.
>   Love, Dad

I was at peace with myself. My son sent a tangible sign of his love and concern. I returned in kind.

Henry Ward Beecher was right: "There is no friendship, no love like that of the parent for the child."

When I finished writing this letter, I had five hours before we would leave for the hospital. I did not sleep. I kept myself busy reading e-mails and writing answers.

One exchange of letters was very important to me. For the past few years, Mark Bailey has been a constant in my life. Mark was a senior in 2003-2004. He is one of the most talented young men I know. Together with Jeff Yedloski, another wonderful student who has been a central part of my life since he entered my seminar room, we worked together on the King's College Capital Campaign project. Jeff produced the animation for the video. Mark built the website, and he accompanied me around the country helping me with many location shoots.

Mark was at my side in Washington, D.C., where we recorded scenes with Captain Patrick Murphy, and he was a big help during our week-long shoot during a recording session with Mike Lewis in Nashville, Tennessee. Mark built the Windsor Park Theater website, and he was a frequent visitor in our home. At some time before midnight, I received a beautiful note from Mark. It meant the world to me.

> Doc:
>   We'll be praying for you during your surgery tomor-
> row morning. Have faith in the medical professionals and

stay positive. You've been through lots of hardships in the last few years and this is yet another hurdle to overcome.

Regardless of the future of the show, put your health and your family first. The legacy of quality programming that you have given this area is simply remarkable. In the world today where the media is only focused on the negative, you have always focused on the opposite by bringing out the positive. This will never change regardless of how many episodes air.

Best of luck tomorrow, if there's is anything I can do to help you or Kitch at anytime, please let me know

God bless, and get well soon,
Mark Bailey

In little more than one hundred words, I opened my heart to this young man who had been so kind and loyal to me during one of the most turbulent periods of my life. Together we had traveled more than 6,000 miles working on projects. I cannot begin to count the number of hours we spent together in my editing studio. Our conversations often ran long into the early morning hours.

I liked this young man, I knew his pain, and I wanted to help him maximize his enormous talent.

Mark:

There were two notes I wanted to receive. One was from my son, and the other was from you. Both came, and I can face what is ahead of me as a happy man.

I love you as if you were my own son, and I have done everything possible to help you in every way that I can. If I make it, we will have more opportunities to learn and grow. If I don't, I will always be on your shoulder helping you deal with what life gives you.

Thanks for the memories, and may good fortune
always be your friend.
Doc

My window of opportunity to record the things that were on
my heart and liberate my soul for what was ahead was dwindling
faster than sand in an hourglass. In the stillness of the morning,
my thoughts turned to Kitch, and a letter she wrote to me earlier
in the evening.

My Dearest Tony:
As you go into surgery tomorrow only know how
much I love you and how many wonderful years we'll
have once you're through this.
You have been and always will be my great love
and hero, so rest assured that while they are working
on your heart, you will be in mine safe and sound and
taken care of until you are all better.
I love you seems inadequate to express what I
feel. Just know you are so loved and always Number
One in my life.
God be with us.
Kitch

This letter was so characteristically Kitch, always the optimist,
always a person with a caring heart, always a person with an understanding heart.

In a few words, she said everything that needed to be said. She
was confident, strong, supportive, and kind. She was the person
who helped me to know what had to be done, with the belief that
it would be done successfully.

Whatever peace of mind I had that morning, it came from the
positive energy and love I felt from Kitch. Throughout all of this,
she was my first priority. I wanted her to be safe and secure no

matter what happened, and I used this interim period to tie up all of the loose ends of life so that would happen.

Six minutes before we left for the hospital I wrote this note to Kitch:

> Dear Kitch:
>
> My heart is filled with love, admiration and re-spect for the most important woman in my life.
>
> I love you for who you are and what you do and how you react, and everything about you.
>
> I hope we have many years to come so we can watch the birds, rescue cats and feed the fish.
>
> If we don't, I will always be with you because our love will never die.
>
> Tony

I honestly believed that together we would make it through the surgery and recovery. Because of her, I wanted to make it through the surgery, with her help I knew I would.

With two minutes remaining until our scheduled departure, I wrote one last letter to my children

> Dear Elena and Tony:
>
> As I make my way to the General Hospital, I want you to know that my love for you is total and com-plete. Your faces, voices and great beauty of heart and soul will be in my mind as my heart is being fixed. I hope they are successful, because I would like to have the opportunity to be your father for a few more good years.
>
> If things turn out well, we will. If they don't, I will always be close by doing what fathers do: loving, protecting, celebrating and caring about you.
>
> Love, Dad

It was 5 a.m., time to leave the place I loved and felt secure. It was time to meet my tomorrow. Unlike yesterday, I left thinking about the words of the Saint of Calcutta: "In ...silence we find a new energy and real unity. God's energy becomes ours allowing us to perform things well."

As I drove the van away from Windsor Park, I took one last look, and I knew I was ready. The transformation was complete. I was content. The silence of the night brought me peace.

The words of the saintly, unpretentious Pope who inspired my generation, Angelo Giuseppe Roncalli, John XXIII, gave me hope: "Consult not your fears but your hopes and dreams. Think not about your frustrations, but about your unfulfilled potential. Concern yourself not with what you tried and failed in, but with what is still possible for you to do."

Whatever was about to happen would now happen in God's time on Dr. Michael Harostock's watch with the help of the people in Operating Room 5 who work miracles every day.

St. Mary's High School

Recording a scene at the temporary memorial in Shanksville, PA

Elena and Jeff with my grandchildren, P.J. and Julia

My family, Tony, Jr., Elena, Jeff and Kitch

Father Andrew J. McGowan, 1959

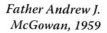

A GOOD DOSE OF
HUMANITY AND HUMILITY

*The person is happiest who lives from day to
day and asks no more, garnering the
simple goodness of a life.*
Euripides

In our house, Dr. Kildare and Dr. Ben Casey had special privileges. To be honest, it was more than that. They were almost divine. In fact, in the year of my birth, 1942, *Calling Dr. Kildare* was produced for the big screen. Yes, that's the same, earnest, caring Dr. James Kildare that entered our home on Thursday evening for five years courtesy of the NBC Television Network. Kildare's competition was another caring medical hero, Dr. Ben Casey.

My mother and father loved these medical dramas, as did my sister. I must admit I liked them as well.

Ben Casey was my favorite. I loved the opening: Man, Woman, Birth, Death, Infinity, five words spoken in a very dramatic fashion while symbols of each were drawn on a chalkboard. It was 1961 TV at its finest.

Casey, a young, intense, no-nonsense neurosurgeon, practiced at County General Hospital. It was his good fortune to have an older, wiser mentor, Dr. David Zorba.

For me, Ben Casey was a medical version of John F. Kennedy's America. In some ways, he was everything I wanted to be: a crusader, a dreamer, and a person who cared about people. Monday evening with Ben Casey on ABC was one of the best nights of the week in our house. It was very compelling drama even when seen on our small, 17-inch, black and white television set.

In our home, the medical profession was held in very high regard. When our family doctor made a house call, it was a big event. Yes, you read it correctly. When Dr. Sloan came to our home with his leather bag, he was always treated like royalty. He was the only person I know who could get the rug in the parlor wet. He never took off his galoshes on the front porch. That was a rule of our house. He was the exception.

Recently, I asked my aunt, my sister, and my cousin a simple question, "What was Dr. Sloan's first name?" No one knew, because he was always referred to with respect as Dr. Sloan.

In the early 1950's, we moved to the Heights section of Wilkes-Barre, and our world changed. It was the biggest event in our family history. My parents bought a white double-block house at 289 East South Street. It was the first home they owned, and conveniently it was right around the corner from Dr. Sloan's office and my Aunt Jean's home. It was also very close to a high school named for the Grand Army of the Republic, a post-Civil War veterans group.

If truth be told, this was a very patriotic neighborhood. The streets were named after Civil War generals: Hancock, Grant, Sherman, and Sheridan. These four men were responsible for decisive Civil War victories at Gettysburg, Vicksburg, Atlanta, and Appomattox. That didn't mean much to me at the time; what mattered was the dirt football field at GAR High School. Every summer we converted it into two baseball fields where we spent most of our days dreaming about the Yankees and imitating the way Mickey Mantle played the game.

The Heights was an ethnically diverse neighborhood before the term became fashionable. Rabbi I. M. Davidson lived across the street. The Charles Leagus Funeral Home was next door to the Rabbi's corner lot. The Kanes lived on the other corner in the shadow of the Patterson apartment building. Marvin Weinstock had a little grocery store that served the neighborhood. The Nanortas lived two doors up the street. John was my age, and his dad was an attorney. That was a big deal. Frank Giering was our tenant. He delivered for the Stegmaier Brewery. Hymie Goichman lived across the driveway from us—a nicer man you never met.

Our neighborhood was host to several special moments every day. When Mrs. Catina wanted to call her twins in for lunch or dinner, she did not use a cell phone. This wonderful woman would open a window or door, cup her two hands on either side of her mouth, and yell at the top of her voice, "Hello Anthony, hello Larry, time to come home."

After dinner, we sat on the front porch on rocking chairs, and we talked with everyone who passed by. My dad loved to talk to the neighbors.

Several times a day we would hear the bells from neighborhood churches, and once a week the eerie sound of the emergency Civil Defense siren made our ears ring.

Once a week, we washed the car in front of our house on the street. It was quite an event.

Several times a week, we would run to my Aunt Jean's house to visit my grandmother. I enjoyed that, because I was one of her favorites. She always had candy, homemade bread, pasta, and pizza for us. No one made pizza like my grandmother.

No matter what the occasion, she would always tell my mother, "Anthony's a good boy." I liked to hear that.

In the fall, we would hear the wonderful sounds of the GAR High School Marching Band led by Richard Ayers. For me, that was a very big deal. I loved the music, the formations, and the marching. I loved the enthusiasm of Mr. Ayers.

The Thanksgiving football game between GAR and Meyers was the biggest event of the year. After the game, we had a formal dinner in the dining room. My mother loved to serve this meal on her "good china." The ritual was repeated on Christmas and Easter.

In the winter, we shoveled sidewalks, and we put ashes from the coal furnace over the ice to prevent people from falling.

In the summer, when it was hot, we put a blanket on the parlor floor, opened the windows, and slept in our underwear.

On Independence Day, there were no fireworks that I can recall, but sometimes we lit sparklers and things called snakes.

When we had a party line, we would listen in on the telephone calls of the other party. Well, at least until my mother caught us, and sent us to our rooms.

Like most of the kids in the neighborhood, we didn't have very much, but we were happy. Our neighborhood was a sanctuary. We knew the people in our world cared about us.

When you ran out of something like sugar, you would go to the next-door neighbor with an empty cup and borrow it. In our neighborhood, everybody shared, because eventually everyone ran out of something.

On East South Street, Mr. Giering always had a homemade pie for us, and a unique way of delivering it. He knocked on the door. When we opened it, he would say, "Hey Bub, here's the rent and some sugar for everyone."

One of the best nights of the summer of 1952 was the evening the Nanortas invited me to go to a drive-in theater with them. What a night. I can't remember the name or the location of the theater, but I do remember the experience. The movie was *The Pride of St. Louis*, a biography of the irrepressible Dizzy Dean.

The fact that Dizzy was a pitcher made it even more special for me. To a kid who never had been to a drive-in theater, it was a larger than life experience.

About the only time I got into trouble was the day I convinced John Nanorta to help me dig up his side yard to build a pitcher's mound so that we could practice. I thought it was a great idea since our yard was but a postage stamp, not big enough for a pitcher and a catcher. His mother didn't agree. John was grounded, and I was banned from the yard.

If you think that no one of significance came from the Heights, think again. In 1917, a youngster named David Bohm was born in the shadow of our neighborhood high school. Bohm graduated from GAR High School in the 1930s. He attended what was then called the Pennsylvania State College. After his graduation, he attended the University of California at Berkeley. He earned his Ph.D. the year after I was born, 1943, and he worked at the Lawrence Radiation Laboratory. In 1947, he became an assistant professor at Princeton University.

The rest is history, and quite a rich history it is including: a classic conflict with the House Un-American Activities Committee, the loss of his teaching position at Princeton, the publication of classic texts in quantum physics, and a friendship with Albert Einstein. David Bohm, an internationally renowned expert on Quantum Theory, was one of us. Much brighter than most of us to be sure, but very much like us in his loyalty to his friends and his traditional values of hard work and generosity of spirit that were central to life in our neighborhood.

In another ethnic neighborhood across town, a precocious youngster was learning about life in the shadow of the Sacred Heart Slovak Church, a monument to Father Joseph Murgas, the botanist, inventor, and radio pioneer. Fr. Murgas is known in our town as "radio's forgotten genius."

This youngster was an only child, a Yankee fan, a Little Leaguer, and a boy who loved to ride his bicycle. Unfortunately, he had an accident that put him in the hospital and eventually in an operating room for a hip surgery. This ended his Little League career, but not his responsibilities at the funeral home his parents operated or his annual trip to Yankee Stadium with his father.

Michael Harostock is eleven years younger than I, but our upbringing is essentially the same. We share a legacy of hard-working parents, devout churchgoers who lived their lives in the service of their family, their church, and their neighbors. They taught values by example, not words, and they expected their children to be responsible, respectful, and reasonable in everything they said and did.

We shared a common heritage, a common neighborhood experience, and a common family experience. We graduated from the same local college named after Christ the King, and we attended Big Ten universities, Ohio State and the University of Iowa.

And even though we never met, our life journeys are quite similar because our parents taught us by example two of the most important life lessons which my mother would have described with these words: "Actions speak louder than words." "You can only go as far as you can push."

When I asked Michael Harostock to share the most important gift he received from his parents, he took no time in responding: "They gave me a sense of home, a sense of family, a feeling that no matter what the situation was, you could always come home." I honestly believe that most of us who grew up in the shadow of World War II can identify with that answer.

On June 12, 2007, the dreamer from the Heights and the thinker from North End met for the second time in the pre-op holding area of the Wilkes-Barre General Hospital. We had a brief conversation before my surgery. I was terrified. He was confident and reassuring. Neither of us knew the exact nature of what was ahead of us. Both of us hoped it would be a good outcome.

On my way to the pre-op meeting and prior to registering, Kitch and I got lost. That's not unusual for us. Fortunately, we met a very friendly and very big security guard who gave us directions with a pleasant smile on his face, and a parting comment that lifted our spirits. As we turned to move forward, he looked at us and said three words that were golden, "Good luck today."

He said it with feeling. He said it with concern. He said it with a reassuring smile on his face.

This act of kindness made me feel very good. To be honest, I was grasping for anything that would calm my fears and give me hope.

Our next stop was the admissions area and another pleasant experience with someone who had been working all night. I don't remember her name, but she impressed me as a someone who was not an "Insurance card and Social Security number" type of person. Believe me, I know the difference. This woman was efficient, but pleasant. I think she sensed my apprehension.

After I registered, another friendly person put me in a wheelchair and took me to the fourth floor where I met Marci Waymen. We had a history of sorts. Kitch and I met Marci after my cardiac catheterization. She is a kind, competent, and caring nurse.

On this morning of high anxiety, she was very good to us. She gave me Intranasal Mupirocin ointment, a treatment that was pioneered at Wilkes-Barre General Hospital and nationally recognized in numerous scientific tests as a procedure that reduces sternal wound infections in open-heart patients.

The Society of Thoracic Surgeons celebrated Dr. George Cimochowski and his team for this discovery: Michael D. Harostock, MD, Robert Brown, MD; Mark Bernardi, DO; Nancy Alonzo, RN; Kathy Coyle, CRNP. This cardiac team won the 2001 Rochester Institute of Technology/USA Today Quality Cup for Health.

On this day, thousands of open-heart patients like me would be the beneficiaries of this procedure. I knew this going into the operation, because our neighbor and friend, Jean Warneka, herself an open-heart patient, gave Kitch a newspaper article about this remarkable achievement.

After changing into a hospital gown, I said my good-byes to Kitch, and I was taken to the pre-op area. It was a large room with sections divided by curtains. It was quiet and cold. I was the only patient.

The silence was broken when Dr. Harostock entered the room. Our conversation was brief but pleasant. To be honest, I don't remember much of what was said. I do remember that he ended the meeting with a joke, a smile, and a promise that he would speak with Kitch before the operation.

He drew the curtains closed, and he left me to my thoughts.

Within what appeared to be seconds, the smiling face of Dr. Jean Emilcar peered through an opening in the curtains. Dr. Emilcar has a beautiful, calming smile and the charming manner of a seasoned diplomat. I connected with him immediately.

Dr. Emilcar is a tall man with a soft-spoken manner and a noticeable French accent. Later I would learn that he was born in Port Au Prince, Haiti, and educated in French schools there before coming to America. He did his undergraduate work at Hunter College graduating with a BS degree in chemistry. He went to medical school at Penn State University in Hershey, Pennsylvania. He completed his formal training in anesthesia at the University of Connecticut in Farmington, Connecticut.

Before the operation, he explained his role as a staff anesthesiologist and an integral part of the project anesthesia team.

Several weeks after the operation, Dr. Emilcar talked at great length with Kitch and me about his specialization:

> The public perception of the anesthesia field is that the anesthesiologist puts the patient to sleep. Putting a patient to sleep is easy, but it's the other things that most people don't see that we do. The job of the surgeon is to be able to fix whatever medical problem with surgery and then our job is to take care of the patient during the operative period. For instance, we making sure that your vital signs are stable, also we make sure that you're under enough anesthesia. At the same time we want to make sure that you don't have too much, because too much would be a problem. So, in a way, we are the internist in the operating room...that means from A to Z we take care of you. If we do a good job, the surgeon will be able to do a better job with his scalpel.

When I asked Dr. Emilcar to explain the secret to being a successful anesthesiologist, his response was very revealing:

> The secret to being a successful anesthesiologist is not only being good with your hands, but also you have to feel for the patient... you treat the patient as if that patient was a family member.
>
> A lot of times we have to be a patient advocate. That means, during the surgery they are not able to make decisions for themselves, so we have to advocate the best decision for the patient. We try to mimic what happens in your body when you are awake. When we do that, there's less incidence of complication like stroke or kidney failure especially in the setting of open-heart surgery. So you could have a successful operation, but if you have any of those complications the operation wouldn't be a success.
>
> Besides putting you to sleep, we have a lot of technologies to let us know how you're doing. For instance, we give you the right amount of anesthesia, and we have some signs that tell us how effective it is in terms of your recall. Remembering what happened in the surgery wouldn't be a good experience.

Dr Emilcar continued:

> Today we have special cutting edge technology to monitor if your brain is being well taken care of. By that I mean if your brain is being well perfused. And then we give the surgeon, Dr. Harostock, optimal operating conditions. We watch your physiology during the bypass operation. We make adjustments, and we keep you hydrated.

Our goal for your particular surgery was to be able to wake you up as soon as things were safe, so that way you don't have to waste any hours of your life lying in a hospital. So we do that by waking you up probably one or two hours after the surgery, so that by the afternoon, you could be awake and talking.

His sense of humor was evident when he told me:
Even though some of your faculties, your mental faculties wouldn't be as sharp as they should be, everything will be intact after the surgery. I wouldn't advise you to sign your checkbook after surgery, but sure enough you could have a meal after the surgery which is extraordinary.

On the morning of my operation, trying to be brave and confident, I asked Dr. Emilcar but one question: "Did you have a good night's rest?" He laughed, and then he gave me a sedative.

After he left the room, a most defining moment occurred. A very tall man with a pleasant way came through the curtains. What I remember most about this nurse assistant was his size and the two razors he was carrying.

Our conversation was brief, and then he went to work removing every follicle of hair from my thighs to my neck, and most of the hair on my right leg and my left arm.

It was a humbling moment. As I lay there watching the symbol of my masculinity be taken from me, I began to realize something about life. Eventually we lose everything.

In that moment, I understood something that is central to my journey: you are not as big as you might think you are. It was a good dose of humility and an incisive indication of what lie ahead. I was not in control of anything but my thoughts, my fears, my hopes, my dreams, and my memories.

A thousand thoughts like this flashed through my mind as I was wheeled from the pre-op room to the operating room. I clearly remember the psychedelic effect of the florescent ceiling lights as the gurney moved along the hallway toward the operating room.

The nurses had been in the room for about ninety minutes prior to my arrival. They were getting things prepared, putting things on a table, getting more than fifty sterile instruments together, and getting equipment together that would be needed for the procedure.

I was barely awake when they pushed my gurney through the door to Operating Room 5. There, I met and had a very brief conversation with Nurse First Assistant, Rose Harlen.

Rose is everything a nurse should be and more. She knows what she is doing, and she cares about what she is doing. She wants to be the very best nurse she can be. She loves what she does, and it shows.

She has given her life to the patients at the Wilkes-Barre General Hospital, and the cardiac team at The Heart and Vascular Institute. She loves being an operating room nurse, and she doesn't complain about the long hours and all of the other pressures associated with the operating room experience.

Service-based people are like that. They are too busy helping others. They don't think about the consequences of their noble behavior, because they are all wrapped up in the truth of their actions. They seek nothing but the silent reward they get when the operation goes well and the patient has a good outcome. They are reliable, responsible, and worthy of our admiration and gratitude.

Rose Harlen is a woman who exudes goodness. She is a woman who personifies honesty and integrity. She is a woman who instinctively does the right thing, because it is the right thing to do. She is a woman who reminds me of my mother and my sister, two nurses who defined nursing for me.

She asked me my name and what seemed to be a dozen other questions, and then I was lifted onto the operating room table.

After that, I don't remember very much as I drifted of into a deep sleep. I do remember the sensation, however, it was like being enveloped by total and complete blackness and silence. It was a very peaceful feeling.

While the nurses finished prepping me for surgery, other members of the surgical team pushed monitors into position. The perfusionist prepared the heart-lung machine. The anesthesiologist put a Swan catheter into the internal jugular vein in my neck, while the nurse anesthetist monitored the drugs that were being administered by IV.

The Swan catheter, more commonly known as the pulmonary artery catheter, is nicknamed "the kiss of the yellow snake" because it is yellow in color, and it is carefully threaded through the right atrium of the heart, the right ventricle, and subsequently into the pulmonary artery.

Named after its founder, Jeremy Swan, an accomplished Irish cardiologist from Sligo, it enables the anesthesiologist to monitor and assess heart functions as well as the effect of drugs during the operation.

The nurses inserted a thin sterile tube called a Foley catheter into my bladder to drain urine which is used for laboratory tests to determine infection, blood, muscle breakdown, crystals, electrolytes and kidney function. They did some additional shaving, and they covered my body with an antibacterial solution. After that, they positioned my body on the operating table, and they draped it for surgery.

Then, Rose Harlen harvested a large section of the saphonis vein from my right leg. The procedure is called an endoscopic vein ligation. This material is used for at least one of the bypasses.

At about this time, my surgeon entered the room. With the assistance of a nurse, he put on his surgical gown and latex gloves taking precautions to keep them sterile. He then made his way to a position where he stood almost 7,000 times before. He paused momentarily to think about the larger implications of what was about to happen, and then he began to harvest a radial artery. In my case, Dr. Harostock acquired the radial artery from my left arm. However, before he did that, he did something that was very telling about him and this operation.

Recalling a conversation we had after my cardiac catheterization when I told him about The Garden of Life in Windsor Park and the words of life that make it so special, he asked everyone in the room to think about a word that speaks to life as they worked on the damaged heart of a teacher who spent a lifetime giving life to his students.

It was a singular moment for everyone in the room. It was vintage Michael Harostock, a man of humility and humanity.

When I heard this story three months after my surgery, I was overwhelmed by the goodness of this man who saved my life. He knew his patient, and he knew what is important in life.

The Scottish writer, John Buchan, was right: "Without humility there can be no humanity."

Dr. Jean Emilcar explains his role in the operation during an interview for our Heart Scene *series*

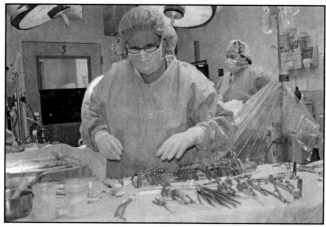

Nurse Rose Harlen checking instruments

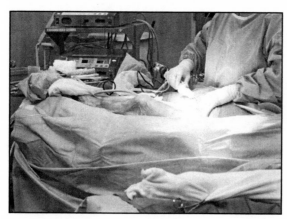

Nurse Rose Harlen harvesting a saphonis vein

THE MIRACLE

Life itself is the miracle of miracles.
George Bernard Shaw

A cardiac operating room looks like the cockpit of a space-ship. At least, that's the way it looked to my untrained eye. There is more visual stimulation in this room than just about any-place I have ever been. It's a place of mystery, magic, and science.

It's a small space with three huge, high intensity overhead lights, no fewer than fourteen monitors, Doppler devices, tables with surgical instruments perfectly laid out in a sterile area, re-frigerators filled with medications and IV solutions, stainless steel rolling carts, white plastic carts holding bright red trash bags for infectious waste, six IV poles, a laser camera on a retractable arm, containers for latex gloves, boxes of white gauze pads, clear plastic bags to hold all of the used gauze pads, supplies of sylastic tubing, and yards of cables. These tools of the trade literally surround the table where the patient lies wrapped and painted with antibacte-rial materials and solutions.

Wherever the eye rests, there is something for the brain to try and figure out.

No fewer than seven people, each with specific assignments and responsibilities, stand or sit in different locations intensely aware of the needs of the patient and the work of the surgeon.

The anesthesiologist and the nurse anesthetist are located at the head of the operating table on a slightly elevated platform behind a plastic curtain. Below them and to the right, the surgeon works on the patient. Across the table, the nurse first assistant and a scrub nurse provide the surgeon with everything he needs.

Behind the surgeon in front a computer with wings, the perfusionist operates the heart-lung machine. A circulating nurse passes equipment onto the sterile field doing a variety of things to move the procedure along without incident.

There is an energy about this room, a poetry about this room, a synergy about this room.

This is a place where competence, caring, and teamwork meet. This is a place where roles are specifically defined and flawless execution is expected. This is a place where the face of the patient is never seen, but the presence and the needs of the patient reign supreme.

This is a place where science and humanity meet to serve the best interest of the patient.

This is a place where miracles of medical science happen every day, yet no one in this room takes anything for granted because everyone knows that this is a place where hearts are stopped for a finite number of minutes so that life can begin anew. According to the experts, 80 percent of all coronary by-pass surgeries are done in the same way my surgery was done, on the pump. Translated into non-medical terminology, my heart was stopped for thirty-six minutes. If that isn't a miracle of science, I don't know what is!

No artist can accurately paint the beauty of this place. No poet can accurately record the majesty of this place.

This is a place where the best that we can be and more happens every day in a quiet, efficient, selfless way.

This is a place where hopes, dreams, fears, and expectations converge in that beautiful moment when a mechanical pump gives way to the repaired human heart. This moment is heralded by three simple words: "off the pump," marking the beginning of a second chance at life and all the wonderful things that come with it.

This moment happens thousands of times every day in hospitals all over the country and the world. In the minds of many, it has become commonplace. Yet anyone who has had the operation or the privilege of witnessing the surgery as an observer like I did knows better. This is truly a remarkable achievement in medical science and a touchstone of human development. From the moment the patient reaches the pre-op holding area, it is 260 minutes of riveting drama, concentration, professionalism, expertise, and teamwork.

I was blessed to experience this procedure both as a patient and as an observer, and as my surgeon, Dr. Michael Harostock, told me, "There is something you know about this operation that I don't. You were on the table, and that is a whole different perspective."

To successfully perform open-heart surgery, it takes a very skillful team of highly-trained and dedicated people working in perfect harmony under the watchful eye of a competent surgeon.

From the moment the door opens and the surgeon enters the operating room, the dynamic of this place changes. In my case, Dr. Michael Harostock came through the door immediately after he finished scrubbing. His hands were raised in front of his chest. He was waving them dry when the circulating nurse helped him get into his blue surgical gown. The gesture continued until he placed his right hand into a specially designed surgical glove. Then he turned his body, and he covered his left hand with a latex glove. These gloves came up well above his wrists to the top of his forearms covering his surgical gown.

Then, he quickly made his way to the operating table, a place he has been 7,000 times before. He adjusted the surgical lights, took his position, and then he accepted an electrocautery device, a hot knife in layman's terms, that separates the tissue electrically and cauterizes the side branches so there's not a lot of bleeding from the vessels that are left behind when the initial incision is made in the chest. This incision begins at the top of the breastbone, the sternal notch, and it continues about twelve inches down the sternum to the xiphoid, about four inches above the belly button in my case.

Then it happened. He was handed an instrument that looks and sounds very much like a jigsaw, and in fewer than fifteen seconds, he divided the sternum by following his initial incision. The whine of the motor is distinctive and very memorable. The moment was incredible and relatively bloodless.

A sterile, stainless steel, retraction system was put in place to force open the chest cavity. This permitted Dr. Harostock to put his hands inside the chest cavity to harvest the left and right internal mammary arteries. Once the internal mammary arteries were harvested, Dr. Harostock used his hot knife to the cut open the pleura, a protective tissue between the ribcage and the lung. Studies have shown that the internal mammary artery has a very successful history. Translated into layman's language, for most patients, this artery holds up very well ten years after surgery.

While this was happening, the anesthesiologist and the nurse anesthetist were monitoring oxygen levels and carbon dioxide levels. They monitor brain wave patterns to determine the depth of the anesthesia. This is very important, because they do not want to underdose a patient. That will result in recall of the operation, a life-altering situation to be sure. They also are careful not to overdose the patient for obvious reasons.

When the lung is exposed, you can actually see the lung breathing with the help of a ventilator or anesthesia machine as it is sometimes called. When the lung is exposed, you know immediately if the patient is a smoker. Dark black spots are visible on the lungs of any patient who is a cigarette smoker. It is just another reminder of human limitations and consequences of human behaviors.

During the procedure, Dr. Harostock and other members of the team frequently check the monitors that are placed throughout the room. These wonders of medical technology record the patient's blood pressure, pulmonary artery pressure, and central venous pressure telling the surgeon and the team how the patient is doing throughout the procedure.

Equally important is a visual check of the heart rhythm recorded on a monitor displaying the results of an electrocardiogram.

From time to time, Dr. Harostock checks the cardiac cath monitor. Located high on a wall above and to the right of the doorway to the operating room, it tells him exactly what needs to be fixed and where the blockages are. This enables him to guarantee that the right procedure will be done for each patient.

Throughout the operation, Dr. Harostock uses a suction apparatus that is hooked up to a cell-saving device that washes and filters the cells, and returns red blood cells to the person undergoing the operation. This is just one of many scientific miracles that helps to guarantee a successful outcome for the patient.

At this point in the operation, Dr. Harostock opens the pericardium, the sac around the outside of the heart. With this accomplished the heart and the great vessels, the aorta and the pulmonary artery, are exposed. What an incredible sight. The heart looks far more delicate and beautiful than any picture I have seen. It is not bright red in color. It is more of a tarnished golden color with a very silky finish. Contrary to popular myth, it is not taken out of the chest cavity during surgery.

Dr. Harostock puts in a series of stitches to make a cradle out of the pericardium. Then, he puts in a series of stitches to hold the various components of the heart-lung machine.

Four tubes from the heart-lung machine go to the heart. One drains all of the venous return from the heart to the heart-lung machine. One of the tubes goes into the aorta, and that returns oxygenated blood back to the largest artery in the body from which all of the other arteries are fed. Another is the arterial cannula for the heart-lung machine. It's attached to the aorta. A smaller tube provides blood flow to the coronary arteries during the surgery when the heart has been stopped.

Heparin, a blood thinner, is administered into the right atrium. It circulates throughout the body preventing the blood from clotting during surgery when it comes into contact with foreign surfaces, like the tubing for the heart-lung machine.

The heart-lung machine must keep the entire person alive while the heart is stopped, and the lungs are not functioning. To do this, it must keep the brain's oxygen saturation adequate to maintain its vital functions. The surgeon wants the heart to be completely decompressed so that he or she will have access and exposure to all the parts of the heart that are required for this surgery.

Dr. Harostock checks to make sure the blood pressure's oxygen to the brain is what it should be, then he puts a clamp on the aorta where the cannula comes from the heart-lung machine so the blood flows through the cannula to the body but not the heart.

For the next sixty plus minutes while the heart-lung machine keeps the patient alive, the perfusionist constantly checks the computer screen of the Medtronic CPB Performer for pressures inside the patient, ratios of blood solutions that are used to bathe the heart muscle tissue, timing devices to let the surgeon know how long the machine has been on, and when doses of medication have been given to the patient. Everything is archived, enabling the surgeon to retrieve the data and compare outcome results.

The Medtronic CPB Performer is an impressive and very complex device. To the untrained eye, it looks like something only Buckminster Fuller could understand. To Dr. Michael Harostock, Dave Burak, and Joe Zimak, it is the best heart-lung technology available.

It stands at attention to the right and slightly behind the surgeon during the operation. Its rich blue and gray color and its brilliant touch screen complete with comprehensive details of vital signs and attention-getting alarms make it a focal point for anyone who enters the OR.

While Dr. Michael Harostock fixed my damaged heart, Joe Zimak made sure that 20 percent of my blood flowed smoothly from the opening in my chest cavity through four sylastic tubes that connected the Medtronic CPB Performer to my circulatory system.

Recently, Kitch and I watched Joe Zimak do the very same thing for a patient who needed five bypasses.

It was a poetic moment, a beautiful moment, a lifesaving moment, an amazing moment, a moment that recorded the genius and the goodness of the human spirit.

It was a moment that recorded how capable we humans are of doing wonderful things, a moment that recorded the highest level of teamwork and some of the most astonishing accomplishments of medical technology and sophistication.

All this is happening while the surgeon looks at the intricacies of the heart through a pair of glasses that magnifies the image 300 percent.

It is sheer beauty and high drama when one of the nurse assistants holds the vein graft that was taken from the right leg while another assistant holds the heart in place as Dr. Michael Harostock sutures the graft in place on the aorta with a hair-like monofilament, polypropylene suture that is barely visible to the naked eye.

In my case, this was repeated four times. After each graft is sutured, the perfusionist injects green dye into the heart-lung machine. This solution makes its way to the graft. Once there, Dr. Harostock inspects the bypass with a laser camera to make sure that it is fully functional.

All this happens with very little conversation between the members of the team, because each person knows what to do and when to do it. It is very much like poetry in motion. In another respect, it is a miracle of science. It is an astounding thing to watch.

For me, watching this procedure while my own body was healing from quadruple bypass surgery was an overwhelming experience. As I recorded the procedure for our *Heart Scene* series, I was stunned by the intricacy and precision of the process. The beauty of the heart amazed me. It is virtually indescribable in shape, majesty, design, and function.

The synergy of the team inspired me, and the competence

and care of the surgeon left an indelible impression that defies explanation.

Like most people, I had no knowledge or understanding of the magnitude of the technology and the skill that is needed to successfully perform this procedure. As I recorded the operation, my eyes were drawn to the hands of the surgeon as they entered the opening in the chest cavity to repair a damaged heart. The most compelling moment happened when I watched Dr. Harostock create a hole in the aorta so that he could connect one of the four bypasses to the aorta.

It was an absolutely captivating scene for me, because I realized at that moment that sure death was being transformed to the possibility of life. There, among a tangle of tubes, instruments, and measuring devices lay the motionless body of a patient who was the beneficiary of this incredible accomplishment of science, medical skill, and human ability. It left me breathless and speechless.

Again and again I thought to myself how fortunate we are to have people like the people in that room trained and available to help us. As I watched Dr. Harostock and his team work in the shadow of the colorful, cerebral oximetry device that recorded the oxygen flow to the brain during the surgery, the word gratitude took on a new and powerful meaning. I was experiencing a miraculous scientific and human moment, and I was changed forever by the experience. I had come full circle from denial to reality, from fear to understanding, from heart disease to heart health, from ignorance to knowledge.

With the bypass grafts in place, inspected, and authenticated, the team begins the process of withdrawing the patient from the heart-lung machine. The tubing that guaranteed life during surgery is clamped. The heart is carefully and gradually filled up, and the 20 percent of the blood that was held by the heart-lung machine is returned to the circulatory system. The heart begins to beat on its own. Dr. Harostock injects medication called Protamine directly into the aorta. It is used to reverse the effects of Heparin. While this takes place, the patient's blood pressure drops slightly.

Final pictures of the connections to the aorta are taken. Four drainage tubes are inserted into the chest cavity and breach through the skin of the lower chest wall to siphon away any fluid inside of the chest that would compress the heart and decrease its ability to pump blood through the system. These tubes are connected to a collection device that allows the doctors and nurses to trend the volume coming from the chest letting them know if there is any internal bleeding.

Seven-gauge wire is inserted into the breastbone in six places to hold the sternum together. The ribcage is pulled together. The wires are twisted, cut, and bent. The skin is sutured together with absorbable sutures, and the incision is painted with a dermabond seal that creates a water-tight dressing.

With this phase of the operation completed, Dr. Harostock meets with the circulating nurse, the perfusionist, and the nurse anesthetist to record data about blood loss and other vital signs recorded during the operation. While this is happening, the nurse first assistant and the nurse assistant prepare the patient for the Cardiac Intensive Care Unit.

The transition from the operating room to the intensive care unit is one of the most critical transitions the patient will make. Dr. Harostock explains it this way:

> It's a very interesting time. The procedure has been completed. There's going to be a transition. It's a well-known phenomenon in surgery that, in fact, bad things more commonly happen during transition periods. The amount of vigilance and monitoring that has to go on at that point is truly inspiring.
>
> The surgery is over. At this point in moving the patient, things can happen. Going from the operating room to the ICU, you're in a hallway on a bed monitoring the patient's heart rate, blood pres-

sure. Making sure that things are uninterrupted for that patient during this move is very important. That's a time when the anesthesiologist, the anesthetist, the nurses, the surgeon accompany the patient from the operating room to the intensive care unit. They need to pay particular attention to a lot of details that were otherwise monitored by an enormous number of computers.

The team of caregivers for any one person passes care of that patient to another team of caregivers in the intensive care unit who have very specific chores. Their duties will include: monitoring heart rate, blood pressure, kidney function, lung function, the recovery of anesthesia and its physiologic effects on heart rate and blood pressure, monitoring and making sure that people don't wake up startled and afraid which will have deleterious effects.

That transition period is critical. The amount of monitoring that is done, the amount of data that's collected during that period of time is enormous. Things can happen very rapidly. Imagine that there's one nurse taking care of one patient, full time at that point, and things can happen so rapidly that, in fact, there's more that can go on than one nurse can take care of.

The seriousness of this transition is recorded on the faces of the five team members who accompany the patient on this journey. As the team moves swiftly, but efficiently, along the hallways and around the corners toward the elevator, there is no loud talking, there is no laughter. The motion of the bed is swift but measured. The anesthesiologist gives the patient ventilation by manually operating the Ambu bag. If ever there was a scene that records the magnitude of what has happened and the urgency of the moment, this is it. It is all competence and focus. It is a synchronous kind of motion that is anesthetizing to watch. It is teamwork at its finest.

For anyone who has had the privilege of observing an open-heart procedure, it is nothing short of amazing. It's a solemn moment. It's a special moment. It's a moment that defies words. It's a moment when excellence is transformed from the realm of the abstract to the world of reality.

As I watched in awe, I realized that my life was dependent upon the skill, the competence, the training, and the execution of many talented and dedicated people.

I realized that a mistake at any point in the process would have very serious consequences. I got an inspirational understanding of how determined these people are to guarantee positive outcomes for their patients. And I began to realize all the things they sacrifice, not only to learn what they must know about this operation, but also to perform the operation at virtually any time of the day or night.

In our celebrity dominated culture, we are inundated with models that, in my opinion, are not the best role models. The people who work quietly and without notice in operating rooms in our community, around our country, and across the world are genuine, real-time heroes. These are the people who sacrifice sleep, leisure time, and family time in order to do what they do, so that people with heart disease get a second chance at life.

We need to put the spotlight on people like the people who are a part of these teams. People who save lives every day. We need to understand the real meaning of the word "teamwork." You know the cliché, "There is no I in teamwork." When you watch people working together in a cardiac operating room, that definition takes on new meaning.

I remember the moment my wife, Kitch, and I walked into Operating Room 5 at the Wilkes-Barre General Hospital. It was a stunning moment. We were overwhelmed by the technology of the place. We marveled not only at the technique, the discipline, the competence, and the expertise of the surgeon, Dr. Michael Harostock and his wonderful team, but we marveled at the atmosphere in the room. It was a bright, cold, active, and very hopeful place. The people who work there are confident and disciplined in everything they do. We've come light years in terms of the technology of open-heart surgery. There are things available to surgeons today that guarantee that this procedure will go very, very smoothly in virtually every instance.

All that being said, it was a very stunning moment for me, because I realized that I was on that table. The things that Kitch and I saw had been done to me. Looking beyond the surface of the human body into the opening of the chest cavity, we stood in awe of the miracle that is each and every one of us. My heart is filled with gratitude for all of the people who helped to repair my damaged heart. In a special way, I have an incredible feeling of gratitude to Dr. Michael Harostock who has been so kind to us from the moment we met. He, more than anyone else, made it possible for us to produce the twenty-one episodes in our *Heart Scene* series.

Because of my experience as a patient and an observer in the operating room, I learned a great deal about life. It was a major transformational moment in my life. I think the person who went into the surgery and the person who came out of the surgery are different persons. The values are the same and obviously the appearance is pretty much the same, but the way I look at life, the way I look at people, the way I evaluate situations has changed dramatically. And I think it's all because of the appreciation for life and a greater appreciation for this miracle called the human body.

Probably the most stunning moment for me in the entire procedure was that moment when I saw the heart beating. There are so many things in life we take for granted and most of them are right here in our own body. If there's any one thing that open-heart surgery does for an individual, at least this individual, it makes you so much more appreciative of all those little things that, in my opinion, are the most important things in life.

With more than 500,000 open-heart surgeries a year, many people look at the operation as just a routine procedure. In fact, some doctors who have performed thousands of these operations refer it a routine procedure for blocked arteries.

In one respect, the operation is an everyday occurrence... routine. During the procedure, the heart is stopped and a heart-lung machine keeps the blood and oxygen pumping through the system under the watchful eyes of a perfusionist, an anesthesiologist, and a nurse anesthetist.

In another respect, it is anything but a commonplace and a rote procedure, especially for the patient.

Nevertheless, the popular culture has a mind of its own, and it defines open-heart surgery as routine. Indeed, a friend once said to me, "Open-heart surgery, it's like just another space launch."

One month after my operation, I received a note from someone both Kitch and I like a great deal. He has been a part of our lives for more than a decade, and we like to think we have been helpful to him in many ways.

On this day, he was writing to us to bring us up to date on developments in his life. His note contained the following words:

> I'm glad to see you're doing well. As I told Kitch when I talked to her a few weeks ago, what you had is routine surgery these days—which is a good thing—and it's good to know you're on the road to recovery. I'm sure you're in good hands.

This came on a day when everything in my body was hurting: the six-inch incision on my left arm, the thirteen-inch incision on my chest, and the smaller incision on my right leg. My stomach hurt from the medication I was taking. The pain in my frozen right shoulder was intense. I was having difficulty with other bodily functions. Nothing was working properly. It was not the best day even though it was one month after surgery.

My response reflected the fatigue and the irritability I was experiencing.

> Permit me one teaching moment. There is absolutely nothing routine about this surgery. When you are sixty-five years old and you know they will rip open your chest cavity.... stop your heart.... put you on a ventilator and fill you with anesthesia that may disrupt your system for months.
>
> The only people who look at this operation as routine are people who do not have to have it. In fact, there is a line from the surgeon that I will never forget. It went like this:
>
> As refined as our techniques are I cannot guarantee a 100 percent success rate. There is a small, but real, possibility that you can die from this operation. In your case, if you look down the road, you are more likely to have a heart attack and less likely to achieve your life expectancy if you leave this hospital without this operation.
>
> Often times the operation is successful and the patient dies from circumstances that are beyond anyone's control. In some cases there are reasons that people will die even if everything is done right by everyone.
>
> A case in point, two infectious disease specialists had to be called in on my case, because there was a positive blood culture which eventually turned out to be contaminated. It was a very scary time, and for two days we did not know if we had a life-threatening infection or something else. Like everything in life, if you

are not in the automobile during the accident it doesn't
look so bad! I do appreciate your attempt to reassure
Kitch, but I must tell you she knew the risks and so did I.

These words speak for themselves. It was a patient's perspective. Yes, there are thousands of these operations performed every day by skilled and very talented surgeons. There are hundreds of thousands of open-heart surgeries performed every year, and I am told that, perhaps very soon, a great number of these operations will be performed by a doctor in front of a computer controlling a robot. That's an interesting scene to contemplate, yet in my mind, and it's the mind of someone who was on the table with his lights out and his heart in the hands of others, open-heart surgery is anything but routine. It is major surgery with major consequences.

Dr. Michael Harostock would be the first to tell anyone that every operation is unique. The surgeon never knows exactly what to expect, because every patient is different.

My nurse first assistant, Rose Harlen, put it this way in her *Heart Scene* interview:

> A lot of our fellow O.R. staff will say, you know, you do the same thing every day, you know, it's open-heart surgery. It's the same thing, never different. And I kind of beg to differ there, because I think it's different every day.
>
> It's a different patient every day. It's a different circumstance every day. So, no, I don't think it's just routine. I don't think any surgeries are routine. I had some personal experiences. My parents came in for routine surgeries, and they were anything but routine. So, I don't ever believe that. I don't like it when people say that.

The bottom line, major surgery of any kind is never routine for the patient. It is natural to have fears, but it is equally important to have hope and a positive attitude. I was very fortunate to have a compassionate and competent surgeon and an experienced cardiac team. Today cardiac operating rooms are places where miraculous things happen every day. I am living proof of that. They are places where damaged hearts are repaired so that people can live the natural length of their life. Yes, there are modifications and life changes that become a part of your new life, but a second chance at life is much better than the alternative.

George Bernard Shaw was right: "Life is a miracle of miracles." I would add but one thing. Getting a second chance at life because of the miracle of open-heart surgery makes the miracle of life so much more meaningful. It's a miracle that helps you learn what is important in life and how to live life in meaningful and qualitative ways. That's what this miracle of science did for me.

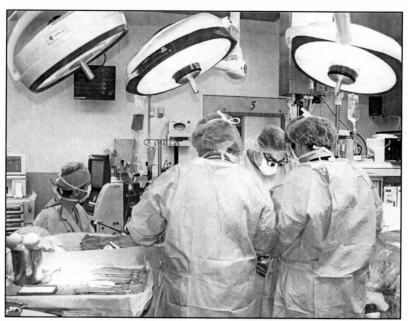

Dr. Michael Harostock and his surgical team

*The Medtronic
CPB Performer*

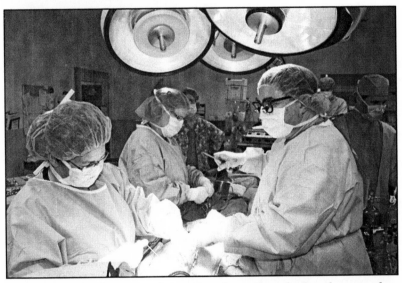

Dr. Michael Harostock suturing the patient during the procedure

*Hospital personnel
get a hospital bed
ready to transport a
patient to the CT ICU*

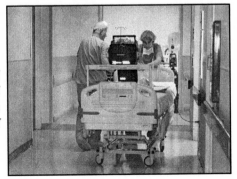

DANGER ZONE

It may seem a strange principle to enunciate as the very first requirement in a hospital that it should do the sick no harm.

Florence Nightingale

The Cardiac Intensive Care Unit is a place where medical technology and bedside nursing meet in the patient's best interest. For the family, it is a place of high anticipation, anxiety, and inquiry. For the patient, it is a time of change, danger, and transition. For the highly trained nurses who work in this special unit, this is a time of careful observation, comprehensive monitoring, and numerous decisions. In the calm and quiet of the Cardiac Intensive Care Unit, hundreds of images and dozens of blood samples record the patient's first steps toward a second chance at life.

Like most open-heart patients, I have no recollection of anything that happened during my twenty-four-hour stay in the Cardiac Intensive Care Unit.

Unlike most open-heart patients, the production of *Heart Scene: A Journey of Discovery and Recovery* enabled me to reconstruct the events that took place in the Cardiac Intensive Care Unit at the General Hospital. Interviews with nurse Nancy Dines and Kitch literally filled in the blanks for me. Because of their help, I have a much better appreciation of what occurred while I made my way from the darkness and bliss of deep sleep to my days of awakening and gratitude after surgery.

Long before a team of doctors, nurses, and technicians maneuvered my bed into the CT-ICU, a highly trained nurse was preparing the room. She checked the cardiac monitor, a sophisticated medical computer. It had no fewer than six cables that would be attached to various points on the patient's body. She attached a number of IV solutions, including powerful cardiac IV medicines, to IV poles strategically located around the patient's bed, and she carefully checked her medications, instruments, syringes, and the ventilator that is positioned behind the patient's bed.

Then it happened. There was a flurry of activity in the hallway. The patient had arrived, and the team began a number of medical maneuvers starting with the anesthesiologist and the nurse anesthetist replacing the Ambo bag with a ventilator. IVs were connected; a portable X-ray machine was wheeled into the room to record images of the chest, lungs, and heart. Then, an electrocardiogram technician appeared at the bedside to record important images of the heart.

The surgeon walked into the room to check the patient, and then he was off to speak with the family members who were waiting in a room separated from the unit by two huge swinging doors.

While this was happening, the nurse prepared the first series of blood samples for the lab, as a constant stream of vital signs appeared on the monitor above the bed.

The cardiac monitor is central to everything that happens in this room. It displays, in real time, the vital signs of the patient: body temperature, the heart rate and rhythm, blood pressure, and blood oxygen levels. Using this information, the nurse adjusts IV fluid requirements and balances the body's intake and output. Hourly cardiac output calculations are done and recorded. This most important calculation enables the nurses and doctors to know how well the heart is functioning post-operatively. The cardiac monitor is the footprint of the patient's recovery. In a way, it's the electronic alter ego of the human heart. What appears on that monitor is mesmerizing.

The most widely known medical device in the room is the mechanical ventilator. Some believe it is the most intimidating device that is required for the patient. If all goes according to plan, the nurse is able to wean the patient from the ventilator within a four to six hours after surgery. In my case, the ventilator was removed in less than four hours.

According to Kitch, my first few hours in the ICU were relatively uneventful except for one issue she described this way: "When I walked into your room and came to your bed, you tried several times to get up. This alarmed the nurses, and they said it might be a good thing for me to leave the room and return later in the afternoon when you had adjusted to the new environment."

Agitation of any kind is not good for an open-heart patient who is on a ventilator and tethered to several IVs.

Kitch left.

I adjusted.

When I first heard this story, all I could think about was my first hospital stay and the great escape attempt, sixty years earlier. Some things are genetic. They never change.

According to my Cardiac Intensive Care Unit nurse, Nancy Dines:

> Patients generally have just a slight recollection of being on the ventilator. Some patients actually have no recollection of being on the ventilator. It's at this time, really, that the patients are at their most vulnerable. They are unable to speak because the breathing tube is in their mouth, and it is connected to the ventilator. One of the biggest fears that patients have is that they will be in pain. It's at this time that we start to give pain medicine if required. We ask the patient if they need it, and although communication is a challenge, we are able to communicate with the patient, mainly by

having them shake their head yes or no to questions we ask as part of monitoring how they're feeling. There's a lot of activity that goes on at this time. We have a one-to-one nurse-patient ratio at this time to make sure that we bring the patient safely through the process. This one-on-one arrangement makes it possible for us to stay at the bedside continuously for the first few hours.

Nancy Dines is a registered nurse. She has completed critical care training and certification. For most of her career, she has been an operating room nurse, specializing in open-heart procedures. Now she gives care to patients after the procedure has taken place. She is competent, experienced, and very much aware of what it takes to be an effective cardiac intensive care nurse. She knows that one miscalculation, one mistake, one poor judgment can have a profound impact on the patient's health and safety. In her words:

> One of the most valuable things a critical care nurse can do to show her commitment to quality patient care is to become certified. That involves passing an extremely challenging exam, and this credential for nurses ensures that their practice is consistent with established standards of excellence in caring for critically ill patients and their families.

In the intensive care unit, there is no room for error, and this can make the life of a CT-ICU nurse stressful. Nancy described it this way:

> The patient is in a very dynamic state when they arrive in the unit after surgery, and we have to

make many decisions very quickly. We have to be able to analyze a lot of information all at one time, and that makes us very good at multitasking.

We view the patient from a holistic point of view, and we want to create a healing environment for the patient and their family, which starts here. We also have to balance that with the technical end of it, and the nurse has to be very technically proficient as well.

When I asked Nancy to tell me what kind of a patient I was, her answer surprised me.

You were an excellent patient. You were very kind, and you were very appreciative of everything that we did for you. It was very nice to meet your wife, as well.

Later she wrote the following note that amplified what she said during our conversation:

When you interviewed me, you asked me what you were like as a patient. I didn't really answer that fully on TV, so I'd like to answer that fully for you now.

I think two things set you apart from all other patients.

As a patient, you were much more inquisitive than most patients are while they're in the CT-ICU. I remember you asked me why I was doing the various things that I needed to do, and you were interested in my explanations. I could tell you were a thoughtful, sensitive person. I feel it's helpful when patients are more engaged, as I feel you were. It gives me valuable feedback to direct my care.

The concern Kitch showed for your well-being was powerful, and I could feel that, and it motivated me further to do my very best for you.

Another thing was that you made an immediate connection with me when I entered the room. I thought that was pretty amazing, that after all you had been through, your good manners shone through. Within a few minutes, you and I were talking about my Irish heritage and your past trip to Ireland.

One word comes to my mind when I think back on that day—connected. Even through the haze of anesthesia, you were connected, to your environment, to Kitch, and to us, the staff.

Thank you again and congratulations on your remarkable achievement, which, when I think about how you both did all of this work, *while recovering from heart surgery,* well, it's nothing short of miraculous!

Reading that note three months after my surgery was a very emotional experience especially the part about Kitch. It brought tears to my eyes, because I was as concerned about her as she was about me.

There is something about this surgery and the possibility that you might be facing death that makes you more concerned about the welfare of those you love. You would think that it would be just the other way. In a self-centered society, you would think that one's thoughts would be all about self-preservation. I can tell you with candor that is not the way it was for me. Yes, I wanted to survive the operation. I wanted to get better and learn how to manage my heart disease, but I wanted that not for me. I wanted life for us.

Nancy's comment about our conversation touched my heart as well. It forced me to relive some of the hopes, dreams, and realities of my life.

When I was growing up, my mother always encouraged me to be myself. I heard that advice in a thousand different ways on a thousand different days. It never resonated with me until I matured and started to become comfortable in my own skin.

When I was a youngster, I never really accepted who I was and where I came from. I came from a tough neighborhood at a very tough time in our history. Political correctness or political sensitivity was not even a blip on the radar screen. Petty jealousies and ethic rivalries were real, hurtful, and debilitating. They caused alienation and division. In the deepest part of my mind and soul, I was never comfortable. I was a part of an ethnic minority, and I always felt somewhat out-of-the-loop.

I always seemed to be one step out of line in what I liked, what I dreamed, what I thought, and what I did with my time.

When I decided to become a college teacher, some of these feelings began to change, but even in that environment, I was never totally at ease. I always felt like an unfinished painting, and I was haunted by the characterization of Theobold in the Henry James' story "The Madonna of the Future." I wanted to make the most of my life and the opportunities it presented. I wanted engagement, action, and growth. I wanted to build things and serve my community.

I did not want to grow old searching for the perfect moment like Theobold. For me, the words of Henry James gave me my canvas: "Live all you can—it's a mistake not to. It doesn't so much matter what you do in particular, so long as you live your life. If you haven't had that, what have you had?"

In the Cardiac Intensive Care Unit as I gradually made my way back to reality, the essential me surfaced: restless, inquisitive, curious, conversational, caring, and respectful. That's the person my parents expected me to be. That's who I was that day, and that was the blueprint for my second chance at life.

When Kitch met Nancy Dines the afternoon of my surgery, she was very impressed by her welcoming manner. Watching her work, Kitch was taken by her skill, dexterity, and precision. She told me more than once that Nancy Dines was a "miracle woman."

With advanced billing like that, I wanted to meet this woman. I wanted to ask her to help us demystify open-heart surgery and encourage people who may have a heart problem to take their first step on the journey to good heart health.

When we did meet three months after my surgery in a room close to where I recovered, I asked her a multi-part question about sensitivity to the patient's needs, compassion for the patient, competence, and expertise to be able to care for the patient.

Her response was immediate and unequivocal: "I agree completely, and I know what you're saying, those are the key elements."

Then she went on to explain her answer:

> We know that patients expect, for example, the correct medicine to be given to them on time. They also expect that they are being given the correct treatment. Those are perfectly reasonable expectations. I have a sense, however, that what the patient perceives to be their biggest need, above and beyond all of the normal expectations, is that the nurse cares about how they are doing. They need to feel that the nurse cares about their well-being, in a genuine and compassionate way. This is my guiding principle as a nurse, that I show compassion to my patients.
>
> It's the most important thing to me. The technical end of things is a given, that I have that technical proficiency, and that I understand what needs to be done and that I'm able to see the big picture relating to the patient's condition. However, I do feel a lot of empathy towards the patient. I could imagine myself in that situation, and I treat my patients the way I would want to be treated.

As Nancy spoke, I could see my mother smiling. That was her credo as well. She learned it early, and she learned it well. In 1928, this daughter of immigrant parents, this woman who was the old-est of eight children, this woman who wanted to be a nurse, this woman who overcame many obstacles to become a nurse received her diploma from the Mercy Hospital School of Nursing. I think June 4, 1928, was the proudest day of her life. Considering the time and place, it was a remarkable accomplishment.

In August 1928, my mother passed her state board examina-tion, and she received an invitation to become a member of the Graduate Nurses' Association of the State of Pennsylvania. She was one of 8,300 members. Each member paid annual dues of $2.50. In addition, each nurse was expected to make two volun-tary contributions: a $1.00 contribution to the American Nurses' Relief Fund and fifty cents to the State Legislative Fund.

Thirty-two years later her only daughter, Mary Claire, earned her nursing diploma from the same school of nursing. I know this was a day of great pride and happiness for my mother.

My mother and my sister personified everything I believe a nurse should be and more. They loved what they did. They took what they did seriously. For them, it was more than just a job. The patients they cared for received their attention, compassion, and re-spect. They were competent nurses with compassionate hearts.

On March 6, 1973, I wrote and broadcast an editorial for the Taft-owned WNEP TV. It was titled "Rules That Don't Work:"

> Sometimes rules and regulations work to the dis-advantage of society. For example, there is a lovely woman we know very well. For the past several years she has been practicing her chosen profession of nursing at a local hospital. Since the death of her hus-band, this has been her whole life, and from what we have been told, she does a rather good job.
>
> This woman is from the old school. Her life is her work. To her patients, she has been an inspiration as well as a necessary part of the complicated medical

process. She is in very good health. She truly enjoys her work, but today she has reached her 65th birthday and the rules say she must retire.

She does not quite understand the reasons why. She does not want to retire, but she must, so she will. This is but one example of how society loses the services of a very skilled nurse. It is symbolic of how the old are pushed aside...their abilities unused.

I know this case rather well because the woman just happens to be my Mother.

Happy Birthday, Mom.

It was a different time and place, but the values my mother lived by then are essential to nursing today.

As Nancy Dines spoke, I heard many of the words my mother used to describe nursing. It was obvious to me that this woman who had experience in Miami, Florida, and London, England, working with open-heart patients and surgeons walked her talk:

It's not a case of where the patient is kind of wheeled in here just to wake up. The patient recovering from open-heart surgery is in a very dynamic state, and during this time we're in close contact with the surgeon. We have protocols that we follow to guide us in our care. And often we need to make these decisions in collaboration with the surgeon, Dr. Harostock. However, we have autonomy within our protocols.

Nancy and I shared similar expectations for surgeons. She expressed hers when she talked about my surgeon, Dr. Michael Harostock:

Dr. Harostock has impressed me as a surgeon. I've worked in four different open-heart programs. I've worked in the operating room in open-heart in Wilkes-Barre, in Miami, and in London. I've seen probably about a dozen cardio-thoracic surgeons in action. I've been a nurse for twenty-two years. I've done open-heart for about fourteen of those years. Now, I can say that I know a good surgeon when I see one. When I saw Dr. Harostock working in the O.R., I was able to see that he is very skilled, very methodical, and he knows what needs to be done. He's very intelligent, very decisive. He is a brilliant man and an excellent surgeon. Dr. Harostock is also a genuinely nice and decent person. Crucially, he is extremely collaborative and respectful to the nurses, which is very important. His behavior facilitates nurses being able to give timely care to the patient. I'm not exaggerating when I say that whenever any of us call him, we just stand right next to the phone, because he always calls us back within about a minute. The relationship between doctors and nurses is crucial to positive patient outcomes. We're fortunate that we now live in times where there is true collaboration between members of the health team. The days of nurses being in the role of handmaiden are well and truly over. This mutual respect has much improved the work environment.

She described my anesthesiologist, Dr. Jean Emilcar, in virtually the same way:

He is a very skilled anesthesiologist. He does an excellent job of taking care of his patients. He's very dedicated to his profession. He is also a very nice person, very respectful, and very much a team player. His quiet, gentle nature puts patients at ease. I'm fond of him."

It was affirming to hear such complimentary words about the doctors who had my life in their hands. Obviously, the first thing I want in medical doctors is competence, but they also have to plug in to the human condition. This thought produced the obvious question. Should the doctors understand the operation from the point of view of the patient?

Nancy Dines agreed:

> I think that as patients become more actively involved as consumers of healthcare, they have high expectations of their doctors and hospitals. If they're not happy, they feel they have the right to go elsewhere. With all the changes that have affected the business side of healthcare, professionals working in healthcare must have good customer service skills, good people skills. This includes physicians. If the patient does not connect with the doctor, they will take their business elsewhere. But it's much more than that, doctors have a deep need to care, to heal, as it were, and I think that the emotional connection that can be formed with the patient is one of the most satisfying aspects of the doctor-patient relationship. It's certainly true for me in nursing. What other profession can offer you that chance to really connect with people in such a profound way?
>
> The job that we do definitely requires a lot of dedication, and you do give of yourself emotionally and physically to do this type of work.
>
> It can be very stressful. When everything's going fine and everything is perfectly balanced

with the patient, it still is stressful, because at any moment, things can change. And if things do take a turn for the worse, we all jump into action and try to solve the problem that has arisen. It can be very difficult emotionally when things don't go as expected. And this is something that nurses and doctors have to deal with.

Florence Nightingale recognized this in the 1850s. She recorded her thoughts about it with these words: "Apprehension, uncertainty, waiting, expectation, fear of surprise, do a patient more harm than any exertion."

She could have been talking about me. Most of the time I was in the hospital, I was apprehensive, anxious, and frightened.

In the days before my operation, I read everything I could find about hospital care. One article, in particular, had a profound influence on my state of mind. It was an article about infections patients contract while they are in the hospital. The numbers speak for themselves. In 2007, a study by Centers for Disease Control and Prevention estimated that 1.7 million hospital patients—4.5 of every 100 admissions—become infected each year, causing or contributing to the deaths of nearly 100,000 people

I was particularly concerned about methicillin-resistant staphylococcus aureus, better known as MRSA infection. "Infections with antibiotic-resistant bacteria such as MRSA, which are difficult to treat, are transmitted primarily by the contaminated hands of health care providers who have touched a colonized patient or something in the patient's environment."

Caregivers who leave the bedsides of such patients without performing hand hygiene may carry thousands or even hundreds of thousands of colony-forming units of antibiotic-resistant bacteria on their hands.

There is a remedy for this. If every caregiver would reliably practice simple hand hygiene when leaving the bedside of every patient and before touching the next patient, there would be an immediate and profound reduction in the spread of resistant bacteria.

The recent, widespread deployment of waterless, alcohol-based hand antiseptics has made this task easier even for harried caregivers. Performing hand hygiene with these products kills bacteria (with the exception of Clostridium difficile) very rapidly, takes much less time than traditional hand washing, and is gentler on the hands than soap. Yet compliance with hand hygiene remains poor in most institutions—often in the range of forty to 50 percent.

At the time of my surgery, this issue was being widely discussed in New York. I knew about the story of Johanna Dailey of Brooklyn who entered the hospital for repair of a routine fractured shoulder in 2004. Within a few days of her discharge, she had a very high fever. She died three months later from a severe infection caused by a combination of deadly bacteria.

The story of Marjorie Parker Hurt resonated with me as well. According to her son, Robin Hurt, she entered the hospital with a broken arm in 2005. She was given a medication she was allergic to. Shortly after that, she caught a hospital-acquired infection, and in forty-eight hours she was dead.

Robin Hurt's campaign to improve safe hand hygiene is recorded at www.washyourhands.org. He told me that a portion of an article written by Dr. Don Goldman of the Institute for Healthcare Improvement is included in the article on this site. Dr. Goldman, an infectious disease specialist, has been an outspoken advocate for higher hand washing standards at all hospitals. He wants to see the day when a patient will not have to worry about this issue.

The Commonwealth of Pennsylvania has launched Clean Hands Saves Lives, a broad based public information campaign using traditional and new media. The centerpiece of Clean Hands Save Lives is a high intensity television commercial entitled "Attack of the Killer Germs." It dramatizes the importance of hand hygiene. Information about this public health campaign is available at www.cleanhandssavelives.org.

Something else I read influenced my hospital behavior. It went like this. You must be your own advocate, and if you can't speak for yourself, you must have someone who will be your advocate.

My life has been a life of questions asked in the classroom, on location, and in the peaceful interview setting of Windsor Park. It's something I've been trained to do. It's something I do naturally. It's something I have learned to do with respect. I was entering a whole new world, and I was frightened. This is a very human emotion, and one that all open-heart patients experience. The Nancy Dines of the medical world and the people who took care of me in the CT-ICU know how to help patients during the anxious moments of recovery. They know that engagement is an effective way to win a patient's trust. They know that taking every precaution including good hand hygiene is in the patient's best interest

What I experienced in the CT-ICU reaffirmed a deeply-held belief. There is nothing more valuable to a patient than a caring, compassionate, competent nurse. Henry James was right: "Three things in human life are important. The first is to be kind. The second is to be kind. And the third is to be kind."

In another part of our conversation, Nancy Dines talked in poignant ways about the human dimension to nursing.

We were recording Nancy's interview in the CT-ICU when the door opened and another nurse politely said, "We need the bed." Two orderlies were at the door to move the bed to the operating room where Dr. Michael Harostock was finishing an open-heart procedure.

We stopped what we were doing, disconnected our equipment, and the bed was removed. Then, we entered the room again to record Nancy as she completed the final arrangements for the patient who would spend about twenty-four hours in transition between the operating room and the Cardiac Step Down unit.

Then it happened. Nancy finished her work, and Kitch asked her the most profound question of the day: "How do you deal with the loss of a patient?"

Kitch knows something about this. As a child of 11 she witnessed the death of her father. The cause of Francis X. Loftus' death was a massive heart attack. He was forty-nine. His oldest child is haunted by that memory to this very day.

In August 2006, she was there when her mother, our beloved Rose, took her initial steps toward heaven.

This year she was with me every step of the way during my surgery and my recovery. She held my hand, less than two months after my surgery, while we waited in line at a funeral home in Nanticoke, Pennsylvania, to visit with the family of Tom Gill, a robust person who had open-heart surgery the same day as my surgery.

Several times during my stay in the step down unit and during my exit examination, our paths crossed. Tom, his mother, Kitch, and I became fast friends.

On a hot and humid evening during the summer, we waited in line with hundreds of people to pay our respects to Tom and his family.

It does not happen frequently. The statistics are clear about this. Less than two per cent of patients do not survive either the surgery or the first thirty days of their recovery. But it does happen, and when it happens, the consequences are immediate and very real.

Nancy Dines explained how she deals with the loss of a patient:

> It is extremely difficult. As a team, we feel devastated. Then as a way to recover from it, I have to take a philosophical view of the situation, and I know that sometimes we can't control everything. We're not in charge of what destiny holds for us. Prayer helps too.

The words Nancy Dines used were powerful in themselves. The volume and cadence of her words were equally powerful. Yet, for me, it was the expression on her face while she struggled to answer the question that said it all.

As I recorded this special moment, my mind wandered to a place I had been several time during this process, and I raised the question that came up frequently during my private moments of thought and reflection: What if I die? What will death be like?

When you face open-heart surgery, or any serious surgery for that matter, the prospect of death becomes a chilling reality.

Questions about life and death are always in the back of one's mind, but they get modified when one experiences the death of a friend or an open-heart patient. Then, the questions are: Why did I survive? What is my purpose? What should I be doing with my life?

Even on the very good days during your second chance at life, you are aware of your mortality, and that makes the value of life so much more meaningful.

When you know you are living on borrowed time, you take full advantage of the opportunities of life.

In my opinion, thinking about the reality of death can enrich life. Things that once were important fade into insignificance. For me, the center of my life is not things. The center of my world is using my time productively for the benefit of others.

Every day presents an opportunity to do something, learn something, give something. The richness of life, nature, and relationships takes on new meaning. Every sunrise is more beautiful and every sunset is more vivid. The little creatures of the world become subjects of great joy.

A note written from the heart enriches a day. An unexpected invitation adds a certain bounce to your step. Genuine friendships with people who care about you and stand with you in difficult times brings a kind of joy that is indescribable.

And when the darkness of night covers the world with its blanket of peace and quiet, you are not paralyzed by the fear of death. On the contrary, thoughts of gratitude fill your heart and soul.

Standing in the Cardiac Intensive Care Unit of the General Hospital, talking with Kitch and Nancy Dines, I realized how precious life is. I realized how beautiful the profession of my mother and my sister is. I realized that nurses like Nancy Dines and Melissa Ulichny, the two CT-ICU nurses who cared for me, are invaluable. I realized that this is a place of medical technology and humanism. This is a place of precision and attention to detail. This is place of quiet competence and caring. This is the setting for a new portrait of my life, a portrait that will be vivified with rich colors of gratitude, respect, and appreciation for what happens in this danger zone every day of the year.

The immortal Gandhi was right. All of us should live as if we were to die tomorrow and learn as if we were to live forever.

Nancy Dines shares a funny story about my stay in the CT-ICU

Nancy Dines talks to Kitch about her work in the CT-ICU

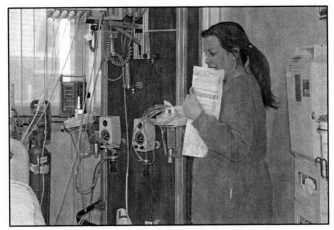

Nancy Dines prepares the room for an open-heart patient

Jane Rose Petro, 1928

Mary Claire Mussari, 1958

FIRST STEPS

God loves to help him who strives
to help himself.

Aeschylus

You may be wondering why I chose to begin this chapter about the first steps of my new life with a quotation from an ancient Greek playwright who lived 525 years before the birth of Christ. Not just any Greek playwright, mind you, but the father of Greek tragedies.

Well, the answer is simple. Without my ever knowing it, Aeschylus was a frequent visitor to my home on Columbus Avenue. In fact, his advice was a cardinal rule of our home. It was modified a bit to read more like Aesop's quotation: "The Gods help them who help themselves."

In our house, my mother modified it to: "God helps them who help themselves."

I heard those words often during my childhood, and they became an essential part of who I am and what I believe. Translated into the language of our neighborhood, we had to become independent. We had to learn how to stand on our own two feet. My mother was quite emphatic about that.

You can imagine what was going through my mind when I found myself in a very dependent state after open-heart surgery. It wasn't a comfortable situation physically or psychologically.

After about twenty-four hours in the Cardiac Intensive Care Unit, two nurses helped me get into a chair with wheels. They put a bag with my belongings on my lap, and they carefully pushed me into the hallway, past the nurses' station, and through the huge swinging doors toward the Cardiac Step Down Unit.

I know this scene very well, not from the memory of my own experience, but from a scene Kitch and I recorded for our *Heart Scene* series. It's a somewhat routine procedure with one exception. The nurses must coordinate the movement of the chair with the movement of the IV pole. That takes a good deal of hand-eye-foot coordination.

The Step Down Unit is an exclusive club, if you will. You must have open-heart surgery to qualify. It is physically separated from other wards, and the nurses and technicians who work there all have special training. Throughout the day and night, a steady stream of medical personnel and hospital staff visit to collect blood samples, administer respiratory therapy, give medication, serve meals, clean the room, and check on your progress.

The room is equipped with a cardiac monitor that records vital signs. There is a bed and a reclining chair. I chose the reclining chair. That is where I sat and slept for five days. Two other staples of contemporary culture, the telephone and a television set, were in prominent places in the room. I chose to use neither during my stay.

My room, Room 7, was located off the beaten path just behind the nurses' station, To my surprise, many people found their way to my door every day.

My surgeon, Dr. Michael Harostock, was usually the first person to visit every morning. His wife, Beverly, was a frequent visitor as well, and his nurse practitioner, Donna, checked in to talk and share information about my situation.

Dr. Harostock is blessed with the qualities of a mensch and the brilliance of a scientist. What I enjoyed most about his visits was the laughter and his willingness to engage in conversation that was not necessarily about my surgery, my heart, or my condition. I got the sense that he was genuinely concerned about the whole person. I trusted him, and I looked forward to his visits. I always felt better after we talked.

My family doctor, Michael Fath, visited every day. He's a pleasant person with an engaging way. His demeanor in the hospital setting is serious and professional. I will always be grateful to him because he was the person who accurately diagnosed the seriousness of my situation, and he is the person who actually got me into the hospital.

Dr. Jean Emilcar, the man who put me into deep sleep, visited regularly. His smile and his welcoming way always lifted my spirits. He was the only physician to sign my Hug-A-Heart pillow, a huge, red, heart-shaped pillow that is used to cut the pain when an open-heart patient coughs or laughs. I have that pillow to this day, and it is a constant reminder that without lifestyle changes, I will be using it again.

Another person who visited frequently was a pleasant man with a kind disposition, my respiratory therapist, Bob Drago.

Bob is a man with a wonderful smile. He greets his patients in a way that makes them feel he is their best friend. He always made me feel like I was a part of his team. He explained everything that he was doing, why he was doing it, and then he would very gently take me through the exercises. I found him to be a comforting person.

After open-heart surgery, you want people to be nice to you, because for the most part, you really don't know what's going on. You're frightened, unsure of yourself, and very sensitive to just about everything. You see all this equipment in the room. You see the nurses and all that they have to do. You want to believe that you have competent people working with you, people who enjoy their work, people who take their work seriously. You want and need reassurance and encouragement from professionals who care about their patients as well.

Bob Drago is that kind of person. He is not an imposing man. He is not a person who draws attention to himself. He is not one to gossip or waste time. Bob is blue-collar solid. For twenty-five years, he has been helping patients, first at Nesbitt Hospital and then at General Hospital when the Wyoming Valley Health Care System was created.

Bob was a student at our community college when his father had open-heart surgery in 1995. That's when he decided to become a respiratory therapist. For the last ten years, he has been walking the halls at Wilkes-Barre General Hospital bringing a smile and quality care to his patients.

He likes his work, and he told me it makes him feel good about himself when he helps someone who is struggling. He also told me that when he enters a room he tries to treat the patient as if it were his mother or father in the bed. He tries to be nice to every patient he meets.

Bob had a very difficult job. He had to get me to use a number of breathing devices that would make sure that my lungs were completely inflated and functioning normally. At first, it was an effort of major proportions to inhale and exhale the steam-like solution from a device we called the pipe. Gradually my body adjusted, and my mind got over its resistance to these exercises.

Joe DeVizia and I have been friends for a long time, almost fifty years to be precise. Our friendship began at St. Mary's High School. When we attended St Mary's, it was the oldest Catholic high school in the county and the keeper of a grand tradition. It was a parish school in a downtown neighborhood and part of a complex of buildings owned and operated by the Religious Sisters of Mercy. Victorian in design, it was located next to a convent and Our Lady of Victory House. Across the street, the workers in a bottling house produced our favorite beverage, Ma's Old Fashioned Root Beer.

When you entered the school, you were greeted with a sign that read: "Be a good Catholic and you will be a good American." In another part of the school, a sign read: "A winner never quits and a quitter never wins." Patriotism and perseverance were central to the St. Mary's ethic.

Like the school featured in the 1945 movie, *The Bells of St. Mary's*, our school had its Sister Benedict in a principal named

Sister Mary Assumpta. Our Father Chuck O'Malley was a young priest named Andrew J. McGowan.

St. Mary's was home to that inspirational teacher named Sister Mary Hilary. She was a no-nonsense, hard working, old school teacher with a very modern sense of the church and its responsibilities. The way she taught, and what she taught changed our lives forever.

The grand red brick building with white Greek columns that was St. Mary's High School is no more. Gone, too, are the other buildings of my childhood schooldays, the convent where I served mass at 5:30 in the morning and the Victory House with its perfectly manicured lawn. Many St. Mary's graduates who became judges, politicians, businesspeople, teachers, doctors, nurses, and priests are gone as well, but Sister Hilary's legacy lives on in people like Joe DeVizia.

During the summers of our youth, we played in a pick-up baseball league every weekend at Penn Lake. Joe's dad was a pharmacist and a community leader. He owned a cottage at Penn Lake. Joe organized the baseball games. Playing on that dirt field was almost as good as playing for the Yankees. I can still remember the people, the spectators, and the innocent fun we had under the hot summer sun playing on our field of dreams.

Today, half a century later, Joe is a respected member of our community. He is the Executive Director of the county's Human Services Department and a deacon in the Catholic Church.

When Joe crossed the threshold of Room 7 in the Step Down Unit, I felt the presence of his goodness and his spirituality. The whole atmosphere of the room changed. It became a peaceful place of faith, friendship, and confraternity. It was the scene of the most beautiful moment of my stay there.

One morning Joe entered the room, and he asked me if I wanted to receive Holy Communion.

I hesitated. He helped me.

I explained my situation with the church.

He responded with a wonderful gesture of reconciliation, and there in the privacy of my room, in the presence of an old and trusted friend, I did what I wanted to do for a long time. I received communion. It was an experience like no other. It made me feel connected with my God. It made me feel wanted by my church. It made me feel whole.

It made me remember the words Sister Hilary spoke to me the day before she died: "When we meet God, we will be embarrassed by his capacity for forgiveness."

For one brief moment, I connected with the traditions of my childhood and everything I had been taught at that wonderful old school. That moment and everything it symbolized will always have a very special place in my heart. I am sure it made my mother and Sister Hilary smile.

My mother would have described this scene with these words: "A friend in need is a friend indeed."

Another St, Mary's graduate who gave me strength is my oldest and dearest friend, Ellen Doyle Mondlak. Ellen and I have been friends and partners since 1955. Together, we danced to rock 'n' roll music at the Friday night dances at the Catholic Youth Center. We drank coffee and cherry Cokes at the Sugar Bowl, one block away from the school. We ate CMPs, sundaes that combined chocolate ice cream with marshmallows and peanuts, definitely not heart healthy according to today's standards, but sinfully delicious to teenagers at the Spa on Public Square, and we got into our share of trouble just by being who we were. Not the serious, malicious things that headline the news today. Our trouble was about smoking in the ladies' room or who threw the cherry bomb at the convent. These were childish things, sophomoric things, innocent things by anyone's standard.

There was never a romantic attraction between us. We were just friends, good friends, loyal friends who knew what friendship was all about. Whatever I did in life, it was always done more efficiently and more effectively when Ellen was with me.

Ellen, her husband, Jerry, Kitch and I have become closer, if that is possible, over the years. It should come as no surprise that the first visitor to Room 7 while I was there was Ellen. Proudly wearing her *Windsor Park Stories* shirt and clutching helium-filled balloons, she came into the room with a smile. She left leaving a cloud of happiness behind.

Not long after, her son, Dr. Jerry Mondlak, was standing next to me talking about his recent surgery admitting that he had orders from his mother to keep tabs on me.

That's who Ellen is, all service and substance, no pomp and circumstance. The daughter of a medical doctor who died at an early age, Ellen is not accustomed to privilege or special attention. On the contrary, she is a down-to-earth, salt of the earth, matter of fact, I'm your friend forever kind of person.

Throughout my hospitalization and recovery, Ellen was a source of inspiration and strength to both Kitch and me.

When fate turned the tables on Ellen and Jerry four months after my surgery claiming the life of their son, the doctor, we were there in every way we could to comfort, console, listen, and support.

Ellen Doyle-Mondlak: mother, businesswoman, community leader, and friend is another jewel in the crown of the Religious Sisters of Mercy who made the St. Mary's experience so special and so lasting.

If my mother were alive, she would say this about Ellen: "A friend is someone who knows the song in your heart, and can sing it back to you when you have forgotten the words."

When Kitch walked into Room 7, it was like someone opening the curtains and letting the sunshine in. She never came empty-handed. She always had a smile that lifted my spirits. In her hand, she carried a sheaf of papers containing e-mails from friends, former students, people who followed *Windsor Park Stories*, and family members.

It's amazing what a few kind words written on a piece of paper can do for someone who is recovering from major surgery. Kind, encouraging, thoughtful words make you feel good all over. They make you forget, at least for the moment, the aches and pains of recovery.

Kitch is a woman who is welcoming by nature, and her story-telling skills were just what the doctor ordered. Shortly before my cardiac event, we rescued a mother cat and her five Maine Coon kittens. It's not the first time we had done something like that. Our two house cats, Regina and Jack, are rescue cats. It's just part of Kitch's nature. She loves animals, and over the years, she has taught me the beauty and calming nature of house pets.

The six Maine Coon cats were now part of our family, and the stories about their adventures in and around the greenhouse and the potting shed took my mind off the things that troubled me, the inability to do things for myself and the fear that somehow I would never be able to regain the high energy levels that served me well in the garden, on location, and in the classroom.

Like most open-heart patients, I wondered if I would ever be productive again, and I feared the prospect of a life of recurrent heart problems. For a person who was groomed to be fiercely in-dependent and resourceful, I dreaded the possibility of becoming a permanent member of the medical establishment arranging my schedule around blood tests, X-rays, stress tests, doctors' visits, and all that comes with it including the paperwork and the insur-ance claims.

Kitch was sensitive to these apprehensions, and she always was encouraging, positive, and willing to help. She was the per-fect partner. Her recollections of life in the Step Down Unit are interesting and quite vivid. She was very taken with three women who helped me take my first steps. This is the way she described them in an episode of our *Heart Scene* series about life in the Step Down Unit:

> Genny Falzone is a rehabilitation nurse. She is just lovely. She's the person you want to have tak-

ing care of someone you love, because she treats them as if you were her own family. Genny literally got you on your feet to take those first steps. Genny always had a smile. She always had words of encouragement. She would say, "You can do it, I know you can and in a couple of days, you're going to feel ever so much better."

Genny would come to your room dressed in colorful scrubs. Her dress matched her personality. She would gently help you up from the recliner chair. She would take your arm to steady you, because in those first few steps, you don't have your sea legs. Those first few steps were difficult, because you hadn't been on your feet in a while. You were wearing those white elastic, anti-embolism stockings with little booties on your feet to keep you warm and the hospital gown. You would tentatively take those steps out of your room. Genny encouraged you to go slowly, very slowly. Together you walked down the hallway toward the exit from the Step Down Unit. She had such a caring way about her.

A second rehabilitation nurse was Colleen Mahon. She's a gentle soul with the most wonderful smile. She also took you for walks, and at some point, you got better and better, and some days you would actually go through the doors of the Step Down Unit and down the next hallway as you got stronger and you got more confident.

Colleen would make the walk a pleasant experience. She always had that wonderful smile on her face, and she always encouraged you and asked you how things were going. She was interested in how you were feeling, how things felt to you, how you were coming along. That kind of caring was really endearing.

The third member of your team was Michelle Merkel, and for some reason, she seemed to be working when I was there, so I got to see her more often. The really nice thing about Michelle was her charming and engaging way. She is a natural at what she does. She is very serious about her work. She knows the things that had to be accomplished, but she always had a nice word for everyone. She always told me how you were doing, what you were going to do, and what you needed to do to go home. There was a calmness and a quiet confidence about Michelle. There was a joyfulness about her, and it was very nice to be in her company.

The nurses were lovely, and they were very comforting, but they also had a job to do, and that job was to make sure that you could walk on your own and come home and manage just fine. They taught you how to walk up steps, because as easy as it sounds to us, it was quite an ordeal after open-heart surgery. Open-heart patients have a lot of discomfort, but they need to know how to negotiate the steps in their homes. It was challenging, at first, because it's the last thing you felt like doing during recovery.

They do their jobs beautifully, and you don't even realize it, because they keep talking and encouraging you and comforting you along the way. And pretty soon you're able to do it on your own.

Kitch's description of Genny, Colleen, and Michelle is right on the dime. We would meet these women again in cardiac rehab.

Kitch was also fond of two of my nurses: Laurie Healey and Sue Kohut. They made her feel welcome. They were polite and receptive to her questions.

During an interview for our *Heart Scene* series, I asked Laurie Healey to talk about my case and her work with Kitch and me during my stay in the cardiac Step Down Unit. This is what she said:

> A few months ago you had open-heart surgery. You had a lot of anxiety over it. We did, however, encourage you that it would get better, and obviously, by looking at you today, that has held true.
> You were a typical patient. You're very anxious after surgery... just a lot of fear about what's going to happen in the future... and as we tell our patients, that it takes time to heal, and you did a great job.
>
> We care very much about our patients. We want to see them do well. We encourage them to walk. We encourage them to breathe. It's very hard at times. Patients have a lot of pain. They don't want to take deep breaths, so you have to make them take pain pills, make them deep breathe, make them walk, even though they don't want to, so it's very challenging as a Two West nurse.
>
> Patients seem to feel that they're cared about, and they're not just a number... they're human beings. We try to treat them as we would like to be treated ourselves.

On the same day, I asked Sue Kohut to tell me about some of the things cardiac nurses have to know to care for their patients.

Her list included: telemetry, monitoring, medication knowledge, and overall assessment skills of patients, to know what's normal, what's abnormal. Cardiac care nurses chart their patients every hour. It's a lot of paper work, but it produces an accurate record of the patients' progress.

When I asked her to describe her job, she was quick to answer with four words: "I love my job." Then she expanded her answer telling me she loved the people she worked with and the patients she served.

From a patient's point of view, Laurie Healey and Sue Kohut were excellent bedside nurses. They cared about their patients. They were very competent. They understood and empathized. They were positive, friendly, helpful, compassionate, courteous, engaging, and always vigilant about the patient's best interest.

They were very comforting to Kitch.

Joan Kondzala was usually an early morning visitor to my room, and in my opinion, she has one of the most important jobs in the hospital. She is a member of the Housekeeping staff. If these people don't do their job well, all kinds of things can happen and they wouldn't be pleasant.

Joan would come in, and she would clean my room as part of her job, but she also stopped and chatted. In our conversations, I learned about her family, and she learned about mine. It was a very pleasant relationship.

She had a unique way of getting her work done, but at the same time, incorporating the patient into the job she was doing. She would chat while she did all kinds of things to make sure the room was perfectly sanitary and in very good condition. I was impressed by her thoroughness. I was taken by her pleasantness, and I admired her work ethic. She took pride in her work, and she wanted to do a good job. Joan is a lovely lady. She goes about her job with such ease and such a sense of accomplishment. She knows the importance of cleanliness. She knows that in a hospital setting, it can all fall apart if the Housekeeping staff isn't doing its job in a conscientious way.

I had one very surprising moment with Joan. The day before I left the hospital, I started to record the names of everyone I met. When I asked Joan for her name and address with this explanation, I want to say thank you to the people who were kind to me in a special way, her face lit up and she replied, "No one has ever done that for me before."

Those nine words spoke volumes, and they reminded me of something Dennis Weatherstone, the CEO of J.P. Morgan, said in a speech I was recording at 60 Wall Street in New York in the early '90s: "In my opinion, the people in the mailroom have the most important job in our organization, because if they don't do it right, everything can fall apart."

When I was twenty-one and in my last semester of college, one of my teachers, Dr. Adam Daryer, said something similar, "If you're going to be a teacher, you had better make friends with the janitorial staff. They know everything that's going on in a school building."

My father was a blue-collar worker, and because of him, I have always identified with people who do the important jobs that no one wants to, the hard jobs, the dirty jobs, the thankless jobs. In my opinion, Joan Kondzala was one of the nicest people I met in the Step Down Unit. She was a model employee and a person who gave me a feeling of safety and security. I am happy she had her moment in Room 7 while I was a resident there.

There were other people who came to Room 7. My sister. Mary Claire, and her husband, Jack, drove from New Jersey to visit. That was a very special moment for me. My daughter came from Virginia, without her children, something she never does, to be with me and to help Kitch. That visit was in a class all by itself.

Tom McGrath, the baby I held in my arms more than fifty years before, visited every day. He is a consummate professional, and a recognized leader in our community. He has never forgotten his roots, and because of that he willingly extended his hand in friendship to both Kitch and me. His smile always lifted my spirits.

One of the doors to the Step Down Unit is the home for a very important sign. Recorded in bold black letters on a pink background, it reads: "All patients who have open-heart surgery must attend a discharge teaching class."

The classes take place in the dayroom outside the unit three times a week. Our class was scheduled at 10 a.m. on Friday. It was a highly personalized event for Tom Gill and his mother, Kitch and me. The dietitian, Cheryl Hartmen, prepared a thirteen-page document that summarized all of the information we would need after our discharge. It included a telephone number if we had any follow-up questions.

As I remember it, I was very tired that morning. I had difficulty processing the information, and I had difficulty staying awake. I think Tom was in the same situation. Kitch was very alert. She took detailed notes. It was a good thing she did, because the information shared in that meeting is vital.

There were a number of life-saving, heart healthy points, a summary of the Ornish Diet, and a number of heart healthy suggestions:

- During the first six weeks of recovery, the diet of an open-heart patient can be high in fat, but not saturated fat.
- Open-heart patients should have three servings of dairy every day, six or more servings of bread, rice or pasta, four or more servings of vegetables, three or more servings of fruit, egg whites, 4 oz. to 6 oz. of poultry and fish.
- It is unacceptable to eat high fat foods like kielbasa or sausage.
- Open-heart patients are allowed 4,000 milligrams of sodium or about 2 teaspoons a day.
- Open-heart patients should not salt food. Products like Mrs. Dash can be used to flavor food.
- Salt-free sodium blends, pepper, garlic powder, or onion powder are examples of seasonings that can be used to improve the flavor of foods.
- After six weeks, open-heart patients should avoid eating red meat. They are encouraged to eat chicken, fish, turkey, tuna, salmon, and shellfish.
- Open-heart patients should carefully watch the cheese content in pizza. They should only eat pizza with low fat cheese.

- It may be advisable to take a vitamin or mineral supplement.
- Open-heart patients should expect a loss of appetite. They should eat small, frequent meals.
- Weight should remain stable. A three pound increase in weight is a warning sign. If that happens, call your surgeon and look for an increase in swelling in the ankles and feet.
- Use Ivory, Safeguard, and Dial soap to shower, and be very careful when washing the chest and arm incisions.
- Open-heart patients must wear their white, anti-embolism stockings for five weeks after surgery.
- Open-heart patients should meet with a home nurse three times a week for the first two weeks after surgery.
- Temperature should be taken in the morning and in the evening.
- If there is any yellow or red drainage from the incision, call the surgeon immediately.
- There will be more pain in the lower part of the incision at first, then higher up. There will be pain across the back of the shoulders and some rib pain.
- Take Vicodin or Extra Strength Tylenol for pain, but not both.
- Daily fluid intake should be a liter-and-a-half a day.
- Five to ten minutes of walking every day.
- Continue breathing exercises.
- Do not drive for six weeks, and do not sit in the front seat of a car.
- Do not lift anything that weighs more than ten pounds.
- Avoid strenuous activity for at least six weeks.

In addition, we received a booklet about cholesterol and a booklet about open-heart surgery.

When the class ended, all I wanted to do was go back to my room and put my head down. For me, it was information overload. Today, I appreciate and understand the value of this information, and I am very grateful we had the class. It was the beginning of the most difficult part of recovery, lifestyle changes.

Before we left the Step Down Unit, a nurse sat down with us to discuss the transition from the hospital to the home. The most important topic was getting the medicines straight. She gave Kitch a sheet of paper with the name of all the medications I had to take, what they did, the time they had to be taken, whether it was morning, noon or night, how they had to be taken...with food, with water, with milk, whatever. For example, I was advised to take a coated baby aspirin, 82 milligrams, just once a day, usually in the morning after breakfast.

The way they did it was especially helpful, because there was an awful lot on Kitch's mind, and she knew that if she didn't administer the medication in the right way at the right time a lot of things could go bad.

Kitch used that paper as a guide until she got so used to doing it that she didn't need it anymore.

The Step Down Unit is a place for rest, rehabilitation, recovery, restoration, and re-entry. It is a place for healing, socialization, and adjustment. During my stay there, I had a lot of time to think about life in the past, present and future tense.

When I was alone with my thoughts, I was filled with an all-consuming sense of gratitude, and I considered a number of ways to express my thanks to the doctors, nurses and hospital staff who were so kind and so helpful during this difficult time. In the early morning hours, when the unit was quiet and all one could hear was the hum of the motors that powered dozens of lifesaving devices, I dreamed about, producing *Heart Scene: A Journey of Discovery and Recovery.*

Every night, thousands of scenes from my childhood to the end of my teaching career flashed through my mind. The sights, the sounds, the faces, and the words of a lifetime painted a picture with several scenes I was determined to change.

In the quiet of the Step Down Unit, words like laughter, joy, family, friendship, work, service, forgiveness, hope, despair, success, failure, love, life, death, legacy, and redemption reverberated in my brain as I reviewed the highs and lows of my life in vivid three dimensional movies in the theater of my heart and mind.

Again and again, I saw and felt the power and the opportunity of three words "Save The Day" brought to life in the music of a dear and trusted friend, Mike Lewis.

I took a trip after midnight,
I know I never left this room.
Woke-up in shadows of moonlight,
and my hands, were shakin' like I knew.

I saw the candles they burned now,
tears they fell on every flame.
In the streets they were cryin,'
saying, things will never be the same.

The flames they grew even brighter.
buildings and bridges that we burn.
I saw you there, in great despair, and I swear,
I know I thought I heard.

Over and over, love will find a way.
Over and over, love is here to stay.
Over and over, love will save the day.
Love, has got to, save the day.

When I was frightened, I managed my fear with a promise to myself that whatever time I had left would be spent in positive ways with positive people who were genuine friends. I was determined to bury the demons of the past and look forward to the angels of the future with hope and confidence.

Done was the time for making something of myself. Now was a time to abandon the joy of achievement. It was time for a new day and a new life. It was time to enjoy the blessings of life after work. The new day of my repaired heart was not something others would manage. It was borrowed time that Kitch and I would enjoy capitalizing on every opportunity to learn, grow, and help others.

It was a new day and the threads of my life were becoming much more obvious to me and to those I loved. I had no idea what lay ahead. I had no idea about the bumps on the road to recovery I would experience, but I was certain that the journey ahead would be different and better. The perspective of heart disease and open-heart surgery taught me lessons about life that were priceless and healing. I was determined to make the most of what I learned. I was determined to save the day.

What I didn't appreciate is the time it would take to fully understand and apply this lesson. My mother was right: "God helps those who help themselves."

A night scene in the Step Down Unit

Nurse Laurie Healey doing paperwork in the Step Down Unit

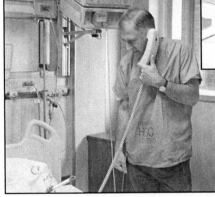

Bob Drago, respiratory therapist

Joe DeVizia makes a visit to the Step Down Unit

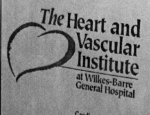

The discharge teaching class poster

COMING HOME

*Few of us appreciate the number of our every-
day blessings; we look on them as trifles.*
John Lubbock

In the summer of 1982, Americans fell in love with a little
boy named Elliot and his friend from outer space, E.T. I remember watching the movie about their exploits in a crowded
movie theater in Connecticut. There, on a beautiful June day
sitting next to my children and Kitch, I was mesmerized by
the story. It was a memorable and very touching experience.

E.T. The Extra-Terrestrial is Steven Spielberg's masterpiece.
Artfully crafted and beautifully portrayed, it's a statement about
life, love, companionship, courage, and decency. It's a moving story
about the power of friendship and the importance of home. ET
touches a sensitive nerve for anyone who knows the frustration
and pain of divorce. For me, it left a lasting impression about the
power of childhood hopes, dreams, and beliefs. In poignant ways,
it reminded me of my own dreams for family and home.

E.T. is rightfully considered to be one of the best movies ever
made. It's also a morality play about the importance of home,
family, friendship, safety, and a sense of belonging. The scenes of
longing and torment, danger and escape, laughter and love left
an indelible mark on my soul.

After six days in the hospital, I felt a little bit like Elliot and
a lot like E.T. I just wanted to go home. Unfortunately, I had this

mysterious and unknown thing in my system, and until the people in the lab and my infectious disease doctors cleared me, I wasn't going anywhere.

Sunday morning, June 17, was an anxious time. It was a beautiful spring day. My daughter was in town. It was Father's Day. I wanted to be with Elena and Kitch in Windsor Park. I worried about what was in the report of the second infectious disease specialist.

At about 10 a.m., we got the word. The test showed that I was free of infection. My stay in Room 7 was over. Without hesitation, I picked up the telephone, and I called home. Unlike E.T., no one was there to answer my call, so I left this message:

"Hi, Kitch. It's me. I can go home if you make contact with me so try and get in touch, OK. Thanks."

Within an hour, we were connected. My things were packed, and we were beginning the ritual that comes with every patient's release. Then it happened. I was sitting in a wheelchair at the nurses' station when I heard the music in the opening of *Windsor Park Stories*. A patient in one of the rooms was watching the program. What a feeling. As I was pushed along the hallway, I could hear the refrain from the opening scenes of the show. It touched my heart. It was a very emotional moment.

When we reached the entrance to the hospital, we had another magic moment. As the valet helped me get into our van, he said, "Now what's going to happen to those wonderful stories you tell on TV?" I was speechless.

The ride home was uneventful. Time passed quickly. Elena and Kitch told stories about their adventures getting the house ready for my homecoming party. There was a new portable air conditioner in a room overlooking The Garden of Life. That's where I would stay. The kitchen was stocked with nutritious, low sodium food. There was a plentiful supply of hard candies on a table in my room next to my recliner. That's what my sister recommended for dry mouth. The refrigerator contained an ample supply of my favorite ice tea.

Once we got home, I slowly and carefully navigated the fourteen steps to the second floor. Without stopping, I made my way to the recliner in my room, and there I sat for a good part of the afternoon. Just being there made me feel good all over. It made me feel safe. It made me feel alive. It made me feel like E.T. in the final scene when the doors of the spaceship closed, and he was back with his family and on his way home.

My daughter figured out how to make the air conditioner work. She set up a baby monitor so that Kitch would be able to hear what was happening in the room. My son called from Ohio, and things settled into a more normal pattern.

The rest of my first day home is somewhat of a blur. Kitch told me I slept a great deal, and she worried a great deal. Alone, with a big responsibility, she was concerned that something might go wrong. There is no preparation for caregiving. It is an anxious time, and some days it is a desperate time.

Being a caregiver for an open-heart patient is not an easy job. Kitch learned that the hard way during the early morning hours of June 18. "I didn't sleep very much," she told me. " I would fall asleep, wake up, and go into your room and check on you. I worried that something might happen. It was a long night. I was scared to death."

If you haven't had a caregiving experience, it's hard to appreciate the conflicting emotions caregivers feel. It's one part Stella, a nurse known for her cryptic comments, who cared for and at times prodded a wheelchair-bound photographer, L.B. Jeffries, in Alfred Hitchcock's 1954 drama, *Rear Window*.

It's one part Frankie Dun, the cold hearted manager and trainer, who shows his humanness when he visits his paralyzed fighter, Maggie Fitzgerald, in the 2004 best picture of the year, *Million Dollar Baby*.

It's one part Hana, the compassionate, romantic, tormented nurse who cares for the English patient in the Oscar-winning, 1996 film of the same name.

It's a very small and modified part of Nurse Mildred Ratched whose oppressive ways managed to alienate everybody in the first picture in forty-one years to win the Oscar for best picture, director, actor, actress, and screenplay in the 1975 film *One Flew Over the Cuckoo's Nest.*

Recovering open-heart patients don't need a dictator like Nurse Ratched at their bedside, but they do need someone who can bring order, structure, and discipline to the caregiving experience.

They do not need a matchmaker like Stella, but they do need someone who will make a commitment.

In another respect, caregivers brings not only their physical selves to the role of caregiving, they bring their psychological selves as well. In Hana, one sees the experiences of a lifetime standing next to the patient. One also sees the elements of circumstance and the humanity of both the patient and the caregiver.

In Frankie Dun, we see how being a caregiver can soften the hardest of hearts. We see how values, or lack thereof, can influence caregiving decisions.

Obviously real life is not like life in the movies, but these examples provide context for the caregiving experience which Kitch once described this way: "It's an imperfect business, this thing we call caregiving."

From my experience as a patient, effective caregiving is both challenging and exhausting. Successful caregiving demands attention, time, compassion, organization, a sense of humor, a sense of proportion, a sense of purpose, a sense of timing, and a sense of spirituality.

It demands physical stamina and emotional balance. The caregiver is both cheerleader and facilitator, caring friend and thoughtful helper, amateur psychologist and physical therapist, confidante, and companion.

It's a human experience complete with all of the fluctuations and vagaries of the human condition and the human personality. There are ecstatic highs and depressing lows. There are moments of fulfillment and times of inadequacy. There are days of progress and moments of regression.

If open-heart surgery is like falling off a building, caregiving is like bouncing off the pavement. Anyone who has been a caregiver will tell you it's not a perfect science. It all about attitude, commitment, preparation, and vigilance wrapped in a blanket of understanding of the patient's needs and the caregiver's needs, as well. It's something that cannot be done alone. It is something that demands connection with family, friends, and professionals.

According to Kitch, it's a little bit of Mary Poppins, but not a lot of the nanny with a spoonful of sugar. It's about superhuman effort, but it's not about a superwoman who gives medication, cooks meals, scrubs floors, does the laundry, cares for the house pets, tends to the gardens, entertains guests, and then goes out and plays eighteen holes of golf with a smile of exuberance on her face and not a care in the world.

Caregiving the way Kitch knew it, both with her mom and less than a year later with me, is not a June and Ward Cleaver activity. There is apprehension, worry, fear, and anger. On some days, it can be too much to handle, and other days it can be a walk in the park.

During an interview for our *Heart Scene* series, Kitch shared her thoughts about her caregiving experience. Her comments were candid and heartfelt:

> Caregiving is difficult. I had to put all my fears in a compartment and keep going on, because somebody had to keep the oars in the water and the boat afloat. I felt that that was my responsibility. So you do what must be done to keep the household moving in the right direction.
>
> I think when you're put in the role of a caregiver, you just look around and say this is what needs to be done. You try to get rid of the lump

in your throat and do it. While you were in the hospital, I felt comfortable because I knew that you were being taken care of by very good, well-trained professionals.

When you came home, I was scared to death, because you had to relearn a whole way of living. I was more or less in charge and had to do the heavy lifting. It was scary, and my heart was in my throat, no pun intended, because if I did something wrong and I didn't keep up my end, then something very serious could happen. You were frightened going into surgery, I was frightened having you come home, because then I really knew that the ball was in my court, and I was on my own.

Having your daughter, Elena, here to bring you home was very helpful to me. She's so competent and she's so level- headed, and she has such a wonderful personality. She is always upbeat, and she made me feel like I could do anything.

She went to the grocery store. She carefully read all the labels to find heart healthy food with low sodium. Whatever I asked her to do, she did it willingly. She was delightful, and she made me feel like I could do what had to be done to help you.

Having neighbors like Jean and Lloyd Warneka who knew something about the experience was very helpful. Jean had open-heart surgery at the Cleveland Clinic. She and Lloyd brought fresh strawberries and chicken pot pies, and they were wonderful neighbors during your recovery.

Rose and Tom Jones were neighbors who cared. Tom had open-heart surgery a few years back, and he knows the territory. He made it his responsibility to cut the grass every week because he knew you could not do it. Rose brought apples in a wonderful bowl. It was such a kind gesture. I have that bowl, and every time I put it on the table it makes me smile.

A former student, Jeff Yedloski, and his dad, Joe, one of your best friends, helped me with the weekly maintenance of the gardens. They did it voluntarily, willingly and their help was a blessing.

Ellen Mondlak helped in every way possible. She brought fresh fruit. She called every week, and she always had a story that made me laugh. She was just wonderful.

Our neighbor, Susan Levinson, sent cards every other day with pleasant, handwritten notes. She volunteered to walk with you when you started your walking program.

Doug McMillan and his son, Adam, drove here from New Jersey, and we had Christmas in July. It was a wonderful day of laughter and happiness. Seeing Adam feed the fish in the garden was a particular delight. His enthusiasm and earnestness were infectious. He named the biggest fish in The Garden of Life, Douglas, after his dad. He called you Opa, the German word for grandpa, and your face lit up. Sometimes the best medicine for a caregiver and a patient is the innocence of a child.

A dear friend from our days at J.P. Morgan, Barbara Hack, visited from New York. It was a marvelous reunion complete with a bouquet of roses and fresh baked goods most of which were not on the approved list of open-heart foods. Together we laughed, told stories and shared thoughts about everything from gardens to politics. We solved all of the problems of the world at our dining room table, and when Barbara left, we both were walking taller because of the gift of her company.

Mike Lewis and his friend, Byron Joyce, the author of *Half-Dead Means You're Still Half-Alive*, came to visit at a time when we needed a breath of fresh air. It was a day that I will never forget. Byron is a skillful storyteller, and he has compelling stories to tell about life and redemption. Mike has been one of your very best and most loyal friends. A frequent visitor to Windsor Park, Mike enjoys my coffee, and he was in a very lighthearted mood as he exchanged quips with Byron. The two friends made us laugh and forget our troubles. Sometimes the best medicine for a caregiver and a patient is a laugh that makes you cry.

There were other friends and former students who came to visit, and every visit gave me respite. It made me feel connected. It brought laughter and joy into our home, and quite frankly, it gave me strength to carry on.

One weekend in July our home was filled with family and friends who attended the annual Irish Teachers Festival in Windsor Park. It was a lot of work to make breakfast for twenty adults and four children, but we managed thanks to a lot of help from our friends, Ann Marie and Frank Pizzani and Ellen and Jerry Mondlak. It's amazing what a caregiver can accomplish with a little help from her friends.

Beverly Harostock, your surgeon's wife, was available and generous with her time. Whenever I was in doubt about something that I thought was important, I called Beverly, and she always made time for me. I never expected that kind of treatment from a surgeon's wife. It humanized the experience, and it helped a great deal.

I was anxious, because I had no medical background. I can't even stand to see a needle put in my arm for a blood test, so this isn't my strongest suit. But I said to myself, you have to do it.

I remember the first time that your nurse, Elaine Blessing, came to set up all the paraphernalia that needed to be set up to record your vitals. There were four devices, and I had to learn how to hook you up to them. It wasn't difficult, but at that point in your recovery, you were still very weak and dependent. After a while, you learned how to do it yourself, but I thought, "Oh, my gosh, I still haven't figured out the VCR, and we're way past VCRs with this equipment. This is going to be very interesting."

I took notes while Elaine explained everything...how to turn them on, how to turn them off, what's good, what's bad. She put all the parameters down on a piece of paper about numbers being too low or too high. She was an exceptional teacher as well as an exceptional nurse. And like everything else, the first time I did it and I got through it everything worked out well. That gave me more confidence to keep on going. Nevertheless, it was an anxious time, and this was one more thing to worry about.

Every day got a little bit less stressful. I think the biggest flaw that I had as a caretaker was trying to be perfect and assuming that I would able to do everything without any help. I wanted to be perfect, and I wanted people to say, "Oh, you just did a wonderful job." Well, ten days after you came home, I went to pieces and cried and cried and cried. I felt very depressed, and I said to myself, "I don't think I can do it." Then everything came crashing down.

Fortunately, your nurse, Elaine Blessing, came here that day, and she told me that what I was feeling was natural. She made me feel comfortable, and I realized that it's okay to be emotional, it's okay to be sad, it's okay to cry, it's okay to be depressed. It's okay to have a lot of the symptoms that the patient has. She helped me to understand that If I repressed my feelings pretending that everything is fine while I tried to do everything perfectly, eventually, I was going to have another meltdown.

So I had my meltdown. It was intense, but fortunately short. When it was over, well, it felt good, and I continued on with the realization that I'm not perfect and I'll do the very best I can knowing that my heart is in the right place.

Kitch summed up her feelings about her caregiving experience with these words:

It's an imperfect business being a caregiver. You're learning on the job. It's a journey with a very important destination, and no user's manual to show you the way. It's a delicate balance of taking charge and taking care of a loved one without taking away their dignity. It can be a lonesome road with many bumps. If you try to be a superwoman, eventually the emotions will come out your ears.

Caregivers need all of the help they can get, and during the first three weeks of recovery, one of our biggest helpers was Elaine Blessing.

Elaine is a Gentiva nurse. Correct that, she is the longest serving, most experience Gentiva employee in our region. We chose Elaine because we had a history with her. Kitch and I met Elaine in 2004 when we were the full-time caretakers for Kitch's mother, our beloved Nancy Beck-Loftus. Well, that's when I thought we met Elaine.

During one of her visits, I learned that many years earlier I met Elaine and her friend, Caprice, in the 1970s at a local television station when she was twelve years old. She and Caprice were volunteers, I was an independent contractor who produced and presented nightly editorials in addition to hosting a quarterly public affairs program, *Town Meeting of the Air.*

It was a chance meeting, but one that left a lasting impression. Life is all about impressions and connections.

For three weeks, Elaine came to our home nine times. She recorded my vital signs like the oxygen levels in my blood, blood pressure, pulse rate, and weight. She examined my incisions, and she checked my ankles for swelling. It is standard procedure for people who have had open-heart surgery. Every day vitals are measured and sent digitally to a location in Florida. From there, they are transmitted to the primary care physician, the surgeon, and the cardiologist.

Kitch and I looked forward to Elaine's visits.

Yes, it was a contact with a person who could answer questions and help us with a variety of issues. Yet, in so many ways, it was more than that.

Elaine is our friend. She is very good at what she does. She is very knowledgeable, and she cares about her work and her patients.

Elaine is a compassionate person who gave us comfort. We felt connected to someone who was available and willing to help us. At the same time, Elaine is a no-nonsense nurse whose values are similar to those of my mother and my sister, both bedside nurses, who were steeped in the old tradition of service and patient care.

There are others like her in the Visiting Nurses Association, but for me, Elaine was the right person for my case.

The monitoring devices Elaine set up during her first visit became central to our daily routine. The first thing every morning was an encounter with a digital scale that spoke to us. The words were always the same: "Please stand still. Please step off the scale. 155.6 pounds."

At 11 a.m., Kitch would open the Gentiva file and record my weight before she helped me with the other monitoring devices. Then we would talk about the numbers and a variety of other issues concerning the operation, the hospital stay, the instructions Elaine gave us for a healthy recovery, and so much more.

When Elaine arrived for her final visit, it was about 2:30 in the afternoon. It was a desperate day for her. She looked exhausted. She was running an hour late, because she was covering for two other nurses who had family emergencies. Her face was flushed, and her clothes were wrinkled from the humidity. Nevertheless, she was cheerful and ready to do her work

After some light conversation, Elaine went to work. She used her stethoscope to listen to my heart, and then my lungs. She checked my incisions to make sure they were healing properly. She checked my ankles and legs for signs of water retention, and then she began to collect the monitoring devices. In the days ahead, these devices would be sterilized and given to other patients.

Sitting in the chair I use when I am working at my computer, she ran through a checklist of items:

- Salt restriction...no more than 2,000 mg a day for life.
- Avoid foods with high fat content and that includes meats that are cured and smoked.
- Use cocoa butter lotion on the incisions. It will expedite the healing process.
- Check your weight every day and your blood pressure and pulse rate three times a week.

- Exercise every day to increase your heart rate.
- Remember you are still in a recuperation period, and you must listen to your body. It will tell you when enough is enough.
- Remember don't cross your legs...don't lift heavy objects, and don't overdo it in the garden.

Then she paused, and shared what she described as the most important lesson:

> You have the body of a 45-year-old man and a heart with arteries that are unblocked. Your progress to date is amazing. For a man your age, your progress has been remarkable. You obviously have a sense of purpose and a will to live.

She paused again, leaning back in her chair, she took a breath and spoke these words: "The most important lesson is this. Don't be afraid to live. You should live the life you want to live."

With these words, an exemplary nurse, a wise person, and a good friend released her patient to the next step in the rehabilitation process. It was a beautiful moment, a touching moment, a significant moment on the road to recovery.

As Kitch and I accompanied Elaine to her car, there was another special moment that I will never forget.

We were walking through the garage. Surrounded by my security blanket, clutter from three-plus decades of teaching and years of production work, Elaine stopped, turned to me extending her arms. When we embraced, she whispered private words that touched my soul: "You are a good man, and I admire what you have done with your life. Continue doing it."

In that moment, I could feel the presence of my mother and my sister. In that moment, I knew I would not be afraid to live.

I was determined to move forward with our *Heart Scene* project, so that Kitch and I could share with others what we learned about heart disease, open-heart surgery, and the journey to recovery. I wanted to open my heart to share some of the things we learned about the caregiving experience.

Nine months later we did just that in two special episodes about caregiving. This is a summary of the ten things we learned:

1. Be open and honest about your emotions.
2. Be firm in your belief that you can do this work.
3. Stay connected to family and friends, they will lighten your burden.
4. Open your heart to your patient. Let the patient know what is going on inside of you.
5. Ask for help with your workload.
6. Seek advice from those who know and have been there.
7. Use the resources that are available to you.
8. Make time each day for yourself.
9. Accept your mistakes and move forward.
10. Always remember, don't be afraid to live. Tomorrow is another day.

In a recent column, Carl Mays, the author of *Winning Thoughts*, quotes the words of Dr. Carl Menninger, psychiatrist and founder of the renowned Menninger Institute: "Attitudes are more important than facts." Many of the characteristics of a positive attitude identified by Carl Mays are essential to successful caregiving. Applying Carl May's words, successful caregivers:

1. Look for reasons to succeed rather than for ways to fail.
2. Accept individual responsibility or develop the philosophy of "if it is to be, it is up to me."
3. Try to grow larger by actually growing and helping the patient do the same.
4. Have good communication skills, especially when it comes to listening to the views of the patient.

5. Understand the importance of being flexible.
6. Take the initiative to accomplish what needs to be accomplished.

If John Lubbock were alive today, he would tell us that successful caregivers appreciate the number of their daily blessings. They know when to laugh, when to cry, when to ask for help, and how to give of themselves to others.

My daughter, Elena, with Kitch

Barbara Hack and Kitch

Mike Lewis and Byron Joyce

Nurse Elaine Blessing examines my incision

*My daughter, Elena,
during her
Thanksgiving visit*

*Kitch with our video equipment after a
shoot for our* Heart Scene *series*

LET'S GET PHYSICAL

The only way to keep your health is to eat what you don't want, drink what you don't like, and do what you'd druther not.

Mark Twain

For most of my life, I've been encouraged to live a healthy life. It started in our kitchen on Columbus Avenue where my mother was very conscious about fat and salt.

She always bought lean meat. She was very careful with salt, and she discouraged anything that would add unnecessary inches to our waistlines. Throughout her life, my mother never weighed more than ninety-eight pounds.

When I was nine, I remember seeing Jack LaLanne on television at my grandmother's house. I was drawn to him because he was small. He had an Italian sounding name, or at least I thought it was an Italian sounding name. Later I learned that he was French. Sometimes nine-year-olds get their facts mixed up.

When I picked up a comic book or a magazine, I saw the muscular figure of Charles Atlas, the man who made a perfect body out of a "scrawny weakling" named Angelo Siciliano. Atlas marketed his "Dynamic Tension" program to "97-pound weaklings" like me. According to those in the know, it was one of the most lasting and memorable advertising campaigns in American history.

The premise was simple, Charles Atlas was for the little guy not the bully. In my teenage mind, he was the personification of masculinity. I wanted biceps just like his. I wanted to do something to get the guys who teased me about my glasses off my back.

Fast forward twenty years. Angelo Siciliano, aka Charles Atlas, died of a heart attack at eighty while doing his daily run on the beach. Jack LaLanne was still pushing healthy eating and healthy exercises on TV. He would continue his television show for fourteen more years. It was the longest running exercise program on TV. For thirty-four years, Jack was in thousands of households every week. After he retired at seventy, he came back into our home via the infomercial. This time he was not pumping iron, he was selling juicers for a healthy body. Almost 700,000 people looking for the secret to a healthy lifestyle bought Jack LaLanne's juicer. Like all things that are too good to be true, 70,000 of Jack's juicers were recalled because of accidents that happened while they were in use.

He was the precursor for a whole army of fitness experts-turned-celebrity. The names and the products are now part of Americana: Jane Fonda's *Workout*, Richard Simmons' *Sweating to the Oldies*, Denise Austin's *Blasting Away 10 Pounds* to name but a few.

The controversial actress and seven-time Oscar nominee produced twenty-three workout videos that **were** sold to 17 million customers. Richard Simmons produced four different *Sweating to the Oldies* videos. They became part of the popular culture in the eighties and nineties.

Even the demure Olivia Newton John dressed in spandex and headband, the dress code of the fitness enthusiasts, got into the act with her 1981 *Physical* video. Who will ever forget the scenes of Olivia Newton John, aka Sandy Olsson, pushing, shoving, and teasing her way through a workout center filled with overweight men. The message was clear. Exercise will make you slim, healthy, and attractive.

But for all of the slogans like: *No Pain No Gain*, *Total Fitness*, and *Working Out*, the exercise boom of the eighties turned out to be a health bust in the nineties. Many from the spandex generation ended up with knee and hip replacements and lower back problems.

The exercise message of the fitness enthusiasts did not resonate with most Americans who refused to accept the premise and the dictum that anything that tastes good is no good for you.

I must admit, I was not a spandex groupie. I never felt comfortable in fitness clubs, and I ate most of the things that were not good for me or my heart. In the eighties, I was a fast food enthusiast. Everything I ate had to have an extra large serving of french fries and a chocolate milkshake. My only visits to a fitness center involved location shoots for video projects. Even then, I did not like the frenetic movement, the loud music, and the sounds of the exercise machines.

You can imagine what was going through my head when I visited the fitness center where my cardiac rehab sessions would take place. I was definitely out of my element.

In September, three months after my surgery, I was authorized by my cardiologist to enter a cardiac rehab program. During the initial meeting with a registered nurse who specializes in cardiac rehab, Genny Falzone, Kitch and I learned that cardiac rehab is an important element in the recovery process.

To be more specific, for an open-heart patient, cardiac rehab is a major step on the road to recovery. Every session has an exercise component. It is designed to strengthen the heart and get it back to its normal capacity to pump blood through the system. Each patient is carefully monitored by a computer device no bigger than a wallet. It is hooked to the waist with a number of wires connected to patches on the chest. This monitor provides real time reports about the vital signs of each patient during the rehab session.

In cardiac rehab, the message about exercise comes through loud and clear.

Exercise helps to improve the heart's function. It helps to improve the vascular system. It also helps to increase your lifespan and your quality of life. It helps the patients improve their strength and their endurance after open-heart surgery.

Daily exercise is essential for good heart health, and it is something all open-heart patients should do for the rest of their life. It's a well-known fact that exercising four or five times a week will help maintain a healthy heart. Brisk walking several times a week is very good for the heart as well. It is also a well-known fact that keeping blood pressure within normal ranges, 120/80, can help prevent heart attack and stroke.

Another element of cardiac rehab is the educational component of the program. Every week the members of the cardiac rehab group meet with an expert in the field: a registered nurse, a counselor, an exercise specialist, a medical doctor, a registered dietitian, or open-heart survivor to learn about the elements of change that are essential for a long, healthy, and productive life. The education program fills in the knowledge gap about heart disease, its causes and consequences while introducing the recovering open-heart patient to a number of lifestyle changes that can lead to a healthy, productive life.

There is one other dimension to cardiac rehab which I think is terribly important, and that's the social dimension.

It's very important for open-heart patients to interact with other open-heart patients. You learn from them, you share with them, and you find out that you are not different from them. The bouts with anxiety and depression, the feeling of impatience and irritability, the challenges with bodily functions and fatigue, and the worry about certain aches and pains are common experiences and part of the recovery process.

Cardiac rehab enables the patient to get these issues on the table for discussion with nurses and specialists who can answer questions and refer them to people who can help. Informal discussions with members of the cardiac rehab group are also very helpful.

Cardiac rehab is a vehicle for connections. There were twelve people in my cardiac rehab group. Ten of them were recent open-heart patients. Two have become very good friends. Knowing them, visiting with them, and talking with them enhances my life in very special ways. I looked forward to being with them during the program, and I try to maintain contact with them and the other members of my group. In the months after my surgery, almost every member of my cardiac rehab group has visited Windsor Park. Their visits have been opportunities for laughter and joy.

The best day was our Celebration of Life Festival, an event we hosted on the first anniversary of my surgery. It was a combination cookout and concert for the members of my cardiac rehab group, the members of the surgical team, and staff members who were part of my heart scene journey. Family members and friends attended as well. It was a glorious day of camaraderie and good will.

Combining exercise, education, and socialization, the cardiac rehab experience is a win-win situation.

My brother-in-law, Jack Doyle, and a an old friend, John O'Brien, piqued my interest in cardiac rehab before and after my operation. Jack told me stories about his experiences in 1998. John related accounts he heard from friends at a health club he attends. Both men were very positive about the value of the program. I was anxious to get started.

On my first day of cardiac rehab, Genny Falzone, a registered nurse, and Michelle Merkel, an exercise specialist, literally took me by the hand to show me the ropes. Their kindness and professionalism helped me through the first day. They made it interesting and much less tedious than I thought it would be. While they measured vitals at every exercise device, they explained what was happening inside my body, how my heart was reacting, and why it was important that I do what I was doing.

Another nurse, Colleen Mahon, sat in front of a computer screen watching computer images and graphs of the other eleven open-heart patients in my group.

Everyone was pleasant and encouraging. They wanted it to be a positive experience. From the first blood pressure reading to the meditation exercise at the end, it was just that, a most enjoyable day in the fitness center.

These three women were part of my rehab team in the hospital. They have a special talent. They have been helping heart patients for years, and it shows. At the very beginning of each session, a nurse or an exercise specialist checks and records the resting blood pressure of each member of the cardiac rehab group. With that completed, every member of the group puts on a specially numbered and assigned monitor. The nurses check each monitor to make sure it is transmitting effectively.

Then a forty-minute session with the cardiovascular equipment begins. There are four different types of machines: treadmills, bicycles, ergometers, and Air Dynes. Some patients even use the rowing machines and the elliptical trainers. The goal is to work the heart muscle and all of the other major muscle groups.

Michelle Merkel, an exercise specialist, knows that the treadmills are probably one of the most popular pieces of equipment. The treadmill is a good overall exercise. It targets the lower body muscles, as well as it being an exercise that is very good for the patient's heart.

The bicycles are popular as well. In my cardiac rehab facility, there were two different types of bicycles: a recumbent bicycle, and an upright bicycle. Both are considered lower body exercises. They are different and work the muscles a little bit differently, however, the patients may choose them, based on their preference.

The U-B-E or upper body ergometer is an exercise machine that works the upper body muscles. This exercise is really important for everyone, but especially for patients who have had open-heart surgery, because they need to rebuild upper body strength following open-heart surgery.

The Air Dyne is actually a bicycle. It is designed to help people build their upper body strength. The pushing and peddling motion is designed to do that.

Each patient works on a machine for ten minutes, then a buzzer sounds, and the patients switch pieces of equipment. If they have been working on a piece of equipment that uses lower body muscles, they switch to a piece of equipment that will work upper body muscles.

During each session, each patient will experience four different machines for a total of forty minutes of cardiovascular exercise, but alternating their muscle groups. Michelle Merkel believes this helps the patient tolerate the session better.

Genny Falzone is the mother of the cardiac rehab experience at the Wilkes-Barre General Hospital. She conducted several of the education sessions. During one of the sessions, "Knowing Your Heart," she explained the intricacies of the heart.

This is a portion of her presentation:

> Our heart, and we only have one, is a muscular organ, and it's a pump, just like the pump on your washing machine. Like a water pump, fluid goes inside, and it's pushed through to the rest of the body. Sounds very easy, doesn't it? But, it's a little bit more complicated than that.
>
> Our heart is divided into chambers, and there's upper chambers called the atria, lower chambers called the ventricles. When you look inside of the heart, you see heart valves. We have four heart valves. They're inside of the heart. There are two on the right side, and we say two on the left side .
>
> On the right side of the heart, we have the pulmonic valve and the tricuspid valve. Now, what they do is open and close to let blood from the upper chambers go to the bottom chambers. On the left side of the heart, we have the mitral valve and the aortic valve.

In another session, she spoke candidly about the importance of aspirin therapy, and how it can save someone's life.

This is a portion of that presentation:

> White blood cells fight off infection. An aspirin prevents those platelets from what we call aggregating or clumping, clotting. So if you think you're having a heart attack and provided you're not allergic or the person is not allergic to aspirin that is a very important treatment to start.
>
> Take an aspirin, and it's probably best if you chew the aspirin, and it goes into your system a lot faster.
>
> It prevents those platelets, because if some of the plaque is broken off, it's hard and it will cause bleeding. When you have partial occlusion of an artery you have a little bleeding there. A clot forms, and when you get a clot there no blood going through, and the person will have a heart attack.
>
> So that is how an aspirin will prevent a heart attack. It prevents that clumping, that clotting, that aggregation of the platelets so that some blood, even if it's a trickle of blood, will help. You still have to go to the hospital, but it will help prevent causing death to that tissue.
>
> And that is how an aspirin can save your life.

Everything Genny said about aspirin therapy rings true with me. On the day of my cardiac event, two Bayer aspirins may have saved my life.

I don't know if my boyhood hero, Charles Atlas, knew about such matters, but he did know something about nutrition. He encouraged his "97-pound weaklings" to be careful about what they ate. Some of his suggestions for healthy life included things my mother tried to regulate in our kitchen at home: caffeine, refined sugar, fatty meats, carbonated drinks, coffee, and tea. Like Atlas, my mother encouraged us to drink a lot of water.

To his credit, Atlas was a big proponent of organic foods. Without question, Atlas and my mother were two people ahead of their time. Obviously their assumptions and life experiences were not rooted in scientific experimentation, but we now have the data. Their nutritional beliefs have value.

Jane Rose Petrozzini and Angelo Siciliano did not know one another, and they probably would not have been comfortable with one another because my mother did not like anything that was offbeat. She was always reminding us not to "show off." The high profile style of Charles Atlas pulling a train, or Charles Atlas flexing his muscles in a leopard skin bathing suit was not my mother's cup of tea. That being said, I think she liked his common sense approach to nutrition.

My mother was a low-profile woman who wanted her children to behave, be respectful, be responsible, and be healthy.

Joan Grossman is the mother of three children. She manages the Cardiac Rehabilitation Program for the Wyoming Valley Health Care System. She is a registered dietitian and an exercise physiologist. She delivered four lectures on nutrition. One of my favorite pictures from these sessions records the moment Joan held up a huge poster of the Food Guide Pyramid with its six categories:

Bread, Cereal, Rice and Pasta Group: 6–11 Servings
Fruit Groups: 2–4 Servings
Vegetable Group: 3–5 Servings
Milk, Yogurt and Cheese Group: 2–3 Servings
Meat, Poultry, Fish, Dry Beans, Eggs & Nuts Group: 2–3
    Servings
Fats, Oils, Sweets: Use Sparingly

Another special picture from my cardiac rehab days shows Joan in front of a PowerPoint image that reads:

Low Fat: 3g total fat per serving
Low Saturated in Fat: 1g saturated fat per serving
Trans Fats: should be "0"

Joan organized a visit to a food market. It was designed to teach open-heart patients how to read labels and how to do heart healthy shopping. It was an important, eye-opening experience for both Kitch and me. We were amazed by the amount of fat and sodium we found in many of the foods we ate, and the products we purchased.

The mantra of this session was simple: "Fat is our first focus, salt is our second focus." Ten words that are undeniably important, but as my mother would say, "They are more easily said than done."

This is a summary of some of the things we learned during our two-hour walk through the food market.

Today the buzzword is organic, but organic has a lot of different definitions. If something is 100 percent organic like vegetables or fruits, it means for at least three years, the farmer or food processor did not use any prohibited fertilizers or pesticides on the fields or pastures where these products were grown. Moreover, detailed records were kept to verify this fact.

Organic food is more costly, because there's a lot more that goes into maintaining organic pastures and farms. No growth hormones, antibiotics, or pesticides are used in the growing process.

Organic will not last as long, so you should buy small quantities of things you know you're going to eat.

When planning your meals, you want them to be power-packed with nutrients.

Patients who are on the blood thinner, Coumadin, should be very careful about the foods they consume, especially dark, green foods. Foods that are dark, leafy green like broccoli, spinach, and kale have a lot of Vitamin K. Vitamin K helps in the clotting process. People who are on Coumadin are instructed to reduce the total amount of dark greens they consume.

Joan was quite specific about the difference between beef and pork. Ounce for ounce, she said, beef has more fat than pork and particularly saturated fat. A comparison of two 8 oz. pieces of meat, one a pork tenderloin, the other a top sirloin, showed that the pork had 5 grams total fat and 1.6 grams saturated fat. The beef had 9 grams of total fat and 3.4 grams of saturated fat.

One complicating factor, the beef had 147 mg of cholesterol while the pork had 95 mg of cholesterol (http://ifitandhealthy. com/pork-vs-beef/)

According to Joan Grossman, beef is not a food that cardiac patients should consume on a regular basis. Three ounces a week is the recommended allotted amount. What is three ounces? It's a piece that will fit in the palm of your hand. It's about the size of a deck of cards or a cassette tape. The leaner your beef is the better.

Small and lean is not a part of the typical American diet. I know that from first-hand experience. Nevertheless, this has not been a challenge for me.

Grilling is much better than baking. Broiling is much better than baking.

Chicken and turkey are the best alternatives for open-heart patients. They are much leaner, not as lean as fish in general. Fish is the leanest from a saturated fat standpoint. But chicken is a great alternative. It's much more economical to purchase, and you can make it in so many different ways, and it's really heart healthy.

Fish is something that's vitally important for cardiac patients and overall general health, but you don't want to eat fish every day because of the mercury content in fish. The current recommendation according to Joan Grossman is three ounces in a thirty-day period.

Lobster, shrimp, and Alaskan snow crabs or king crabs are high in cholesterol, but it's not the cholesterol that we focus on from a dietary standpoint. So, these are foods you can enjoy.

Juicing is really a wonderful thing for anyone who has the time and the inclination to prepare the drinks. That's not Jack LaLanne speaking; it's Joan Grossman talking to our cardiac rehab group.

For someone who is very busy and doesn't have time to juice, super foods like Bolthouse juices and Naked juices are healthy alternatives. They are expensive, and the trick is to use a little. Let a little go a long way.

Super foods like the juices mentioned above have a lot of carbohydrates. One serving has 41 grams of carbohydrates. Someone who is diabetic might want to consider taking a little bit, filling the rest of your glass with water. You still get the value of the good nutrients that are in these super foods.

From a heart healthy standpoint, pomegranate is one of the new foods on the market. Although it's been around for many years, it has made a surge to the commercial market. Pomegranates and blueberries are supposed to be very heart healthy. You want to be careful of added sugar. If you look at the ingredients, the ingredients on the labels are listed in descending order, according to weight. So whatever is listed first has the highest amount of ingredients. Whatever is listed last has the least amount. What you want to look for in juices is no added sugar.

Pomegranate Flavor Juice Blend from Concentrate is a staple in our house. It has no fat, 35 mg of sodium, total carbohydrate 38g, sugars 37g. We take a 64 fluid ounce bottle, and we pour half of it into another container. Then, we fill both bottles with water. That way a two-quart bottle becomes half pomegranate juice and half water. To me, it tastes great. My wife and I drink it in small portions. One bottle lasts a week.

For snacks, I eat a lot of unsalted nuts. Why? Because I learned in cardiac rehab that the omega-3 fatty acids found in nuts are excellent heart healthy fatty acids. They help to keep your vessels pliable and flexible.

During our tour of the food market, I asked Joan about my addiction to a popular brand of ice tea. This is what we discovered.

This 16 fl. oz. drink has lot of sugar, a whole lot of sugar, 34 grams and 40mg of sodium, not a lot of salt. It has 15 mg of caffeine. The sugar comes from high fructose corn syrup. Joan told us there's a great debate right now about high fructose corn syrup. It's early data, but some believe it alters liver metabolism.

We should know how many calories and how much caffeine and sodium is in a drink. The caffeine and sugar dehydrates the body. You don't want that to happen, because that may cause blood pressure to rise.

What a discovery. What a moment. In the middle of the food market surrounded by shoppers who were making choices for themselves and those they loved, most of them, like Kitch and me in this instance, did not know the deleterious effects of these choices. We were trying to make heart healthy choices, and in some cases were making poor decisions.

According to Joan: "Sugar dehydrates the body, and water to the body is like oil to a car." Dehydration is not a good thing for recovering open-heart patients.

Because of this visit and the things I learned, I replaced the popular drink with plain water.

Toward the end of our visit, I asked Joan straight away: "What is the message you're trying to get across to people who are care-givers for open-heart surgery patients?"

Her answer was brief and to the point:

> People need to really understand what to look for, and if you have the knowledge behind what it is that you're looking for, then that empowers you to really make good choices. It's hard work. You've got to get into the grocery store; figure out what are the good choices, what changes you can make and then put those chang-es into action. You have to read, read, read.

Kitch's response to the food market tour was equally frank:

> I would say I've been successfully thrown under the bus several times today. I thought I knew an

awful lot about nutrition and about labels and about right choices, and I don't think anybody can really keep up with the data and the research, but you do have to make the effort. You do have to set aside a time to go to the supermarket and to really read, read, read, and you can't cut corners. You really have to pay attention to what you're eating. You also have to bite the bullet and say I can't eat that anymore, and I know why, and I have to learn to change my palate so that the sugar and the salt cravings eventually leave the body.

In retrospect, I look at cardiac rehab as a place where important lifestyle changes begin. It is so much more than a series of cardiovascular exercises. It's an opportunity to learn in a congenial atmosphere with highly trained professionals and open-heart patients who share common experiences and concerns. It is a place of friendship, community, and growth. If you get it right in cardiac rehab, you are well on your way to the fundamental lifestyle changes that are necessary to maximize your second chance at life.

It's something that cannot be done easily or without help. It is important to involve the caregiver in the educational sessions because as my mother would say, "Two heads are better than one."

Darwin was right: "It's not the strongest of the species that survives, nor the most intelligent. But the one most responsive to change."

Thoreau was right: "Things do not change. We change."

Several members of our cardiac group work out on the treadmill

Genny Falzone, one of our cardiac rehab nurses, checks my blood pressure during an exercise

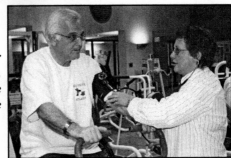

Michelle Merkel, our cardiac rehab exercise specialist, has a special moment with Louie Bigiarelli

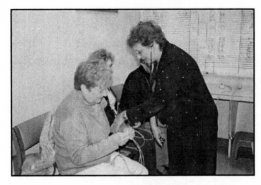

Tina Aufiero checks her monitor with help from Genny Falzone

Joan Grossman, a registered dietician, teaches our cardiac group the secret to a heart healthy diet

Michelle merkel checks Lenny Skibicki's blood pressure at the end of a cardiac rehab session

13

DEMONS WITHIN

If you bring forth what is within you, it will save you. If you do not bring forth what is within you, it will kill you.
The Gospel of St. Thomas

For most of my life, I have lived with the twin demons of anxiety and depression. For a very long time, I did not know them by name, only by experience. When I was a youngster, the worst infection you could get was whooping cough. Where I grew up, anything else one could handle with lots of spaghetti sauce.

When I was a teenager, the universal solvent for anything that bothered you was a shower, preferably a cold shower.

The problem was our home did not have a shower. If truth be told, I was twenty-four years old before I lived in a place with a shower. By that time, I was young, recently married, and a first-year college teacher living in Cedar Rapids, Iowa. I taught four different courses. That meant four different preparations three times a week. I was studying for my Ph.D. at the University of Iowa where I spent most of my spare time. When I wasn't in Iowa City, I volunteered in the congressional office of Congressman John C. Culver in Cedar Rapids.

It was a busy time, a challenging and uncertain time. I was anxious and overstressed most of the time. A worrier by nature, and an overachiever by birthright, I wanted to do well. I was willing to work hard to do well. I dedicated almost all of my energy in the quest for success. In my mind, that's what I was supposed to be doing. I was building a career that combined education and public service. I was oblivious and unconcerned about the consequences of my stress-filled life.

In the 1960s, doctors prescribed either Librium or Valium for what ailed me. They were the new 'Wonder Drugs.' Commonly known as tranquilizers, they helped people deal with the stresses of life. They were the magic bullet for anxiety. I tried both. Unfortunately, they did not work for me. All they did was cause every gland in my body to swell.

One morning I looked in the mirror to find my lips five times their normal size. This traumatic experience made me apprehensive about putting any chemical into my system for many a year to come. I was convinced I could control things with more discipline.

For the next thirty years, I did it the old-fashioned way. I toughed it out. In the parlance of our culture, it may have been the manly thing to do, but it was not the most effective thing to do.

Strategies that are part ego, part fear, and part ignorance never work.

Fast forward to 2003 and beyond. In some respects, it was the worst period of my life, and these two demons tormented me virtually every day of the year. At home, we were caretakers for Kitch's mom. Without question, it was the right thing to do. It was one of the best things we have ever done, but it was a lot more challenging than we anticipated.

In the classroom, things were changing as well. A new generation of students and teachers were much more into technology and the digital age than those of us who learned our craft in the 1960s.

At the same time, the role of the teacher was changing as well. The authoritarian figure, the wise person with the answers or at least the right questions was giving way to a facilitator-type figure who always did the politically correct thing in a student-centered culture.

Older, experienced teachers were looking over their shoulders, as it were, at a new style of teacher skilled in an edutainment culture. Students were involved in every decision, and helicopter parents were placated as well. Overextended by a number of things including the production of major video projects in addition to the rigors of producing *Windsor Park Stories*, I was constantly on the go and not very peaceful or happy.

I wasn't sleeping well. I lost my appetite. At times, I was unable to concentrate. I was questioning my relevance, and I was very sensitive about issues of respect and recognition for years of service. It was a new time and a new set of priorities, and I did not feel connected. There were more highs and lows, and I no longer enjoyed the things I always enjoyed. I was struggling. I was defensive. I was burned out. I wasn't feeling well, but I refused to recognize the obvious. I thought if I worked harder things would get better. They didn't.

I agonized about my future, and after months of soul-searching, I decided to give up the thing that I loved, the thing that defined me, the thing that I looked forward to every day. I decided to resign and leave the place I called home for forty-one years. It was the best decision and the worst decision I ever made. In some respects, it haunted me every day. It was as traumatic as the death of a family member. It initiated a period of isolation and sadness unlike any I have ever known, and it opened the door for the demons of anxiety and depression.

On the advice of my family doctor, I tried an antidepressant for a while. It put me in such a state that I could not function. I refused to have a stress test, and my medical insurance provider refused to authorize payment for a medication I needed for a gastrointestinal problem.

To make matters worse, the sleeping problem I had was diagnosed as sleep apnea. A mild case to be sure, but sleep apnea nevertheless.

So I returned to my die-hard solution of hard work and self-discipline wrapped in a quilt of avoidance and denial. I began a period of feverish activity that was designed to preoccupy every waking minute of every day. Very much like the character in Francis Thompson's poem, *The Hound of Heaven,* I was fleeing down the nights and down the days and in the midst of laughter, I was hiding or attempting to hide great anguish and pain.

After my retirement, Kitch and I traveled to Norfolk, Virginia, for a change-of- command service for our friend, Admiral Sally Brice-O'Hara. There, we recorded scenes for *Windsor Park Stories.* Then we drove to St. Paul, Minnesota, to produce episodes for our *Miracle Project* about the 1980 U.S. Olympic Hockey Team. We returned to St. Paul for the first Herb Brooks Foundation Gala and more location shooting. In December, we drove to Chicago for the induction of Herb Brooks into the United States Olympic Committee's Hall of Fame, and more location shooting. On the way home, we stopped in Ohio, to visit with my daughter and her family. There, we produced a program about my granddaughter's Christmas play. On the way home from Ohio, we managed to get stranded on Interstate 80 in a snowstorm. We were too exhausted to do any shooting.

Looking back, it is obvious that this whirlwind of activity was designed to kill the pain of loss and perceived failure. On the outside, I looked fine. On the inside, I was a veritable mess. There were times when every bone in my body ached, and every memory of the seminar room where I taught brought a Niagara of tears.

The nighttime hours were the worst. I could not sleep. I had vivid and sometimes frightening nightmares. I was angry, heartbroken, and struggling mightily. I made mistakes in judgment. There were times when I overreacted to perceived hurts. I was oversensitive to just about everything. If truth be told, I was crying out for help, because the pain was so great. There were so many burned bridges, so many missed opportunities because no one was listening.

In the midst of all of this, we changed the broadcasting address for *Windsor Park Stories* from public television to commercial television adding a whole new set of challenges. Then, the worst blow of all; Kitch lost her mom. It was a desperate time.

I knew I was in trouble, but the only solution I knew was to put my head down and keep working. That strategy only added to the stress that eventually caught up with me on Memorial Day 2007.

Why I did not die that day will always be a mystery to me. The doctors say that it was because my heart was so strong. I think it was the effective use of aspirin therapy. Whatever the case, the cardiac event led to a catheterization and that, in turn, led to quadruple bypass surgery.

One of the many things Kitch and I learned during my discharge teaching class was to expect bouts of anxiety and depression. My visiting nurse, Elaine Blessing, reinforced that message during her first visit. That was not good news. I knew these two guys intimately, and I knew what they could do to me.

How could I recover from major surgery and deal with these twin demons as well?

The answer was very easy. During the first three weeks, they never showed up. My recovery moved along smoothly, without incident. Could it be that the thirteen-inch opening in my chest gave them an escape route?

Not exactly. It's more accurate to say they went on vacation for a while, but they were not gone for good.

They returned just in time to attend the Irish Teachers Festival six weeks after my surgery. When I saw the crowd, I welled up. When I talked about my former teacher, a person who saved my life, the tears flowed again. When I eyed my wife, daughter, and grandchildren in the crowd, there were more tears. It was a Kleenex evening, and it followed the script that post-operative depression experts warned me about.

At the end of the evening with my blood pressure and pulse rate skyrocketing from the excitement, I had an unpleasant experience with a friend. It happened in nanoseconds, and it came almost without warning.

A perceived slight and a minor volcano erupted. It was as if I were two people standing there, and for a moment, my emotions were out of control. It was an unpleasant moment, an embarrassing moment, and a moment that with a little discipline and a lot of what some call seeing positive intent in others could have been avoided.

A short time later, my demons paid me a call in an even more dramatic way. This time I was sitting in front of my computer screen reading an e-mail. Something I hoped would be in the text was not there, and it sent my blood pressure and pulse rate soaring.

In warp speed, I let my emotions guide my judgment, and my fingers fired off a short, caustic reply. There was little doubt that my two companions were here to stay.

What is so baffling about this incident is that it happened on one of those days when everything seemed to be going well. There were many pleasant e-mails. I was making progress on a project that was long overdue. The weather was glorious. The sun was high in the sky, and The Garden of Life was filled with robins, gold finches, a few hummingbirds, and one or two mourning doves. The sounds were peaceful and very pleasant. Life was good.

I received a beautiful get well present from an old friend from the college, Andy Ewonishon. One of my very favorite people, Julie Marvel, responded to our Windsor Park Newsletter with words of kindness and encouragement.When the mail arrived, there were two inspirational thank you cards with handwritten messages that were thoughtful and affirming.

Memories of a very encouraging visit at the hospital with my surgeon, Dr. Michael Harostock, the day before added an extra bounce to my step that morning. The day was off to a wonderful start, and it looked like clear sailing ahead, or at least that's what I thought.

Like too many days during my recovery, however, I was doing too much. That's always been a problem for me. I need to be busy, productive, involved. I am happiest when I have more on my plate than I can handle. It drives Kitch nuts, and it isn't very good for a person with a healing heart, but it honors the childhood dictum to make the most of my time.

My editing suite is belowground, and I was moving between the editing room and the place where I write. Every change of place involved descending and climbing fourteen steps. I had made that trip several times during the morning.

Then it happened. I was racing between two locations…writing and reading two different e-mails, and my old demons paid me a visit. It wasn't pleasant, it wasn't peaceful, it wasn't warranted, and it wasn't me.

If the event wasn't terrible enough, the sense of guilt and remorse that followed was even worse.

This is one part of open-heart surgery that patients don't like to talk about. It's one of those "in the lodge" affairs. The patient knows it exists. Family members and friends know it exists. Physicians know it exists, yet few patients feel comfortable talking about the anger, anxiety, and depression that often accompanies open-heart surgery.

Quite honestly, I didn't believe it when I read about it prior to my operation or when I was cautioned about it after the operation. Now I am living it and doing the best I can to cope with it.

One of the most positive things about the surgery for me was an increased sense of gratitude, and a feeling that many things I once thought to be important were just not that essential for a happy, productive life. In my mind, I was better able to sort out what really was worthwhile.

I should have known better than to believe I would not experience both anxiety and depression at some point during recovery.

It comes out of nowhere, and it manifests itself in many different ways, but the result is always the same. In my case, there is a sudden increase in blood pressure and pulse rate. There is a feeling of abandonment, then anger which is usually followed by harsh thoughts and words, and then remorse and embarrassment. All this eventually turns into sadness, or at least it did for me.

Some say that depression in recovering heart patients can be the result of the deep anesthesia one must have for this operation. Others dismiss that saying that new anesthesia drugs do not produce that effect. Some believe it is a result of the need for a ventilator. Some think it is all physiological. Others say it is purely psychological.

It is important to note that it does not happen to every open-heart patient. Some believe that it does not happen to the majority of open-heart patients, and others argue that it happens most frequently to open-heart patients who have had issues with anxiety and depression before the surgery.

It can get a little confusing especially for caregivers who have more than they can handle with the physical care of the patient.

Kitch was preoccupied with all of the household chores, taking care of our two household cats and six rescue cats, the fish in three ponds, visitors, correspondence, and a host of other things. Even though she was aware of the possibility of postoperative anxiety and depression issues, she was not prepared for the sudden arrival of my demons. We were in new and turbulent waters.

We were told that many open-heart patients experience mood swings and feelings of anxiety, anger, and depression. It happens after major surgery. When open-heart patients get together, they talk about anger, anxiety, depression, fear, and a sense of helplessness. That's why it is so important to be connected with open-heart patients, because they understand these demons in very real ways. They also know that eventually things get much better.

All I know is that it happened to me, and it was not a pleasant experience. I was fine one minute, and then I would well up with tears the next minute. I would be laughing one minute, and then suddenly my mood would turn to sadness. In some respects, the anxiety was much more pronounced. It always has been, and it was much more difficult to control.

During this time, something else was happening that was very disorienting. I was having the most horrible nightmares of my life. The scenario was always the same. I dreamed that I was in a life-threatening situation with no way out, and just before the bus, or the train, or the violent criminal would take my life, the movie ended. I awoke with my heart racing and a general feeling of fear and alarm.

It was an experience that I was not prepared for, and one that I would never want to repeat.

When I was a child, I had nightmares. In different periods throughout my life, I had similar experiences, but never did I dream anything like the terrifying scenes in these nightmares.

After what seemed like an eternity, but was only about two months, the nightmares ended. The anxiety and depression became less tormenting. As I got stronger and became more accepting of my new life, the medication, the doctors' visits, the blood tests, the lifestyle changes, and retirement, things got better.

In some respects, I wrote and produced my way to recovery. With every article I wrote for the Windsor Park Theater, I learned things about life, the operation, and the healing process. The affirmation that came after the broadcast of each episode of *Windsor Park Stories* was encouraging. These are but three of the life sustaining notes Kitch and I received:

> Just had the pleasure of catching your Sunday show. It made me feel as though it was thirty-five years ago at King's. You were doing more than telling your story, you were teaching. I have a little insight to your surgery story because my wife is the lead nurse with the O.R. Heart team at Geisinger Wyoming Valley.
>
> Just wanted to let you know how great I thought the show was. I hope that I can share your thoughts on life with my children. It may be easier for me to understand at 57 than it will be for them as twenty

somethings. Again glad to see that you are feeling well and still teaching

—**Bill Lisman**

Doc & Kitch,

Today's story was beautiful and a wonderful way to end the series. It was also a real tear-jerker.

I can certainly relate to what you said and felt. Life is very bumpy and not the bowl full of cherries I thought it was as I grew up. There is a lot of work, heartache, pain, and sorrow. But that is life. You can't dwell on it because it makes you bitter. You must learn to accept your plight and move on. I always try to keep that in the back of my head. Congratulations for a job well-done! Have a wonderful week.

—**Virginia**

Kitch and Tony,

Thank you for a great series. You shared a lot of wisdom through your pain and also great love and compassion. I really love all your shows especially your interviews of wonderful people. I know it renews my faith in mankind and I always feel uplifted after watching your programs. I will pray that you continue on this important journey for selfish reasons. I know you are touching lives you may never meet. Isn't God awesome in how He reveals Himself in us? Keep up the great work.

Gratefully,

—**Joanne**

P.S. I hope you take a much deserved vacation again for selfish reasons because I know you're going to get all kinds of ideas for new shows!!!!!!

Dear Tony and Kitch:

I can't say enough about the final program. It made me reach back and reassess some of the things that happened to me and how to better deal with them. I'm sure you and Kitch are very tired mentally, physically, and emotionally from this 21-episode production. People will never realize the work, time, and dedication that went into this series. The both of you can be very proud of this wonderful series. I know I got choked-up myself several times as you related the final five lessons knowing that the series was coming to an end. I really think now you can put closure to your days in the classroom. New doors of opportunity and a new life await you both. Enjoy some time off and bask in some well earned praise for Heart Scene. I have some pictures for you and Kitch when I see you. Looking forward to your next project. Your students would be proud of you both. A job well done!!!!!!!!!!

—Bill Gaydos

The completion of the *Heart Scene* series was a moment of great celebration and relief. Many of our close friends, most of our underwriting sponsors, and many of the people we met at the General Hospital accompanied us to the television station for a picture and a presentation of the final episode. After that, we came together for a cocktail party and reception hosted by Dr. & Mrs. Michael Harostock. It was a joyful day, and one Kitch and I will never forget.

These notes from two nurses captured the spirit of the day:

OH MY GOSH TONY!!!! I had such a wonderful time seeing you and Kitch—the two of you just radiated the love of life—and you both look fantastic. I have said this before so stay with me—the joy and happi-

ness—on so many emotional levels—the awakening
to life, to miracles, to sadness and happy endings—all
that you have brought to my life is simply a reflection
of ALL your unselfish labors, sharing your journey,
and being steadfast and true to who you are. The
Loftus-Mussari venture is the REAL DEAL.

It was a great time at the reception. Tina is just
wonderful—I love her to pieces!!!!! The Harostocks—
well—what else can be said about their gifts—
another great husband-wife pairing. True humani-
tarians. You enjoy your R&R. You smell those roses
along the way Tony—and just enjoy every minute
of it—you and Kitch worked so hard for as long as I
can remember............Celebration of Life—funny thing
is—as wonderful an event it will be—you and Kitch
already have it mastered on a daily basis....God bless
my friend-—I bet hearing your name even gives God
butterflies!!!

love you both!!!

—**Lorraine**

DEAR FRIENDS, YOU KEEP THANKING EVERYONE
WHO HAS HELPED YOU DURING THIS RECOVERY
JOURNEY, WELL I WANT TO TURN THE TABLES AND
THANK YOU! THERE ARE NOT MANY WHO WOULD
SACRiFICE SO MUCH TIME TO SHARE SO MUCH OF
THEMSELVES WITH OTHERS, BY LETTING PEOPLE
KNOW OF YOUR STORY OF RECOVERY,YOU ARE HELP-
ING OTHERS TO ACCEPT AND DEAL WITH THEIR OWN
FEARS AND CONCERNS.

YOU NOT ONLY SHARED THE MEDICAL SIDE BUT
THE EMOTIONAL SIDE OF A LIFE ALTERING EPISODE
IN YOUR LIFE. THIS IS NO EASY TASK. MIKE AND
I HAVE BEEN BLESSED IN OUR LIVES WITH MANY

GOOD FRIENDS, AMONG WHICH ARE TWO VERY
SPECIAL PEOPLE, TONY (DOC) AND KITCH, LOVING
SOULS THAT HAVE BROUGHT THE LOVE OF COMMU-
NITY TO A BRIGHTER LIGHT FOR US. SO THANK YOU
FOR BEING YOU, THANK YOU FOR WHAT YOU DO FOR
THE COMMUNITY, AND THANK GOD FOR KEEPING
YOU HERE TO CONTINUE HIS WORK HERE ON EARTH.
I WAS VERY PROUD OF BEING PART OF YESTERDAY
AND THE TURN OUT JUST PROVES ONE THING ....
YOU ARE LOVED.

—EB

One thing is certain. Support, patience, and understanding from family and friends are vital. Just because a person looks well does not mean that the person is well. You cannot read pulse rate and blood pressure on a person's face. People who are prone to anxiety, anger, and depression are masters at masking these demons. No one wants to appear weak, dependent, and needing help. To be quite honest, real men don't eat quiche. They do eat lots of spaghetti sauce, and that's the problem. Most men are conditioned to tough it out. They will not ask for help, because they see it as a sign of weakness.

In my case, talk therapy has always worked. Being connected with friends and family members who understand and care is essential.

Like so many things in life, if you don't reach out for help, you won't get it. If the medical experts don't get your help in finding what's wrong with you, they can't fix it.

These vital lessons I learned from Bob Hapeman, the person who gave me an EKG in the Cardiac Intensive Care Unit.

Whoever wrote the Gospel of St. Thomas, was right: "If you bring forth what is within you, it will save you. If you do not bring forth what is within you, it will kill you."

A special moment from my last class

Julia, Kitch and my niece Emma enjoying the Irish Teachers Festival

The Connemara Dancers performing at the Irish Teachers Festival

My dear friend Ellen Mondlak serving desserts at the festival

A group of gardeners visit Windsor Park during a garden tour three weeks after my surgery

Joanne Galvin presents the National 911 Remembrance Flag to Windsor Park during the Irish Teachers Festival

LOOKING FORWARD

A man's mistakes are his portals of discovery.
James Joyce

Somewhere between my junior and senior year in high school, I started to read books. George Orwell's *Animal Farm* was a short and a fun read. I loved the message, the style, and the characters. I loved the one liners that satirized the Russian Revolution of 1917 and all things totalitarian. In my youthful mind, this book was about as good as reading would ever get.

With I finished *Animal Farm*, I picked up Orwell's masterpiece,*1984*. I followed the journey of Winston Smith and Julia with the intensity of a disciple. To this day, I have very vivid memories of Orwell's description of the Ministry of Truth, the Thought Police, Doublethink, Newsspeak, Groupthink, Big Brother, and the infamous Room 101. I was hooked on political satire. I would be forever suspicious of reformers who wanted people to sacrifice personal freedom fo bureaucracy and efficiency.

Looking Backward, Edward Bellamy's utopian novel published in 1886, was my next journey into a world of change and promise. Erich Fromm, author of the *Art of Loving*, called Bellamy's portrait of life in the year 2000 "one of the most important books ever published in America." If nothing else, it proves beyond any doubt that Edward Bellamy was a man who was way ahead of his time.

Bellamy's book records the story of Julian West, a young man who falls into a deep sleep and wakes up in a new and changed world with a new structure and several of the modern conveniences of our present world: credit cards, warehouse stores, and cable telephones. Central to *Looking Backward* is a changed social and political order that was controversial then and would be controversial today.

In many ways, an open-heart patient is very much like Julian West. We are put in a drug-induced, deep sleep, and when we wake up, we find ourselves in a new world. In my case, I think it is a better world of appreciation, opportunity, and perspective. The challenges of heart disease, open-heart surgery, and recovery have helped me to see things more clearly. I don't look back. I don't worry about yesterday. I don't take things for granted, but I don't take them too seriously either. I try to learn what I can, and do what I can to help others every day. I stay in touch with members of my cardiac group because that keeps me grounded.

Last evening I spoke with two open-heart survivors who are frustrated and unhappy, but they are not about to give up. One person was just about at the end of her wits with low energy levels and fatigue. Nevertheless, she was looking forward to the weekend and two ethnic festivals, the Kielbasa Festival in Plymouth, Pennsylvania, and the Annual Homecoming Picnic at St. Mary's in Mocanaqua, Pennsylvania. The other person, my friend Louis Bigiarelli, is struggling with a serious infection. He just finished a hospital stay of eighteen days to drain fluid from his lungs. To complicate things, he has prostate cancer. Prior to his hospitaliztion, he was taking radiation treatments.

If anyone has reason to be discouraged, it is Louie, yet he refuses to think negatively. As we were about to end our conversation, he said this: "I must learn to help myself. I must contribute something so that my wife is not doing all the work."

These conversations got me thinking about the things that helped me to look forward with hope and optimism during the days after my surgery. There were several, and they made this book and my journey what it is.

If I were to summarize my thoughts about recovery and the underpinnings of my new life, I would use these words: family, friends, help, laughter, luck, meaning, purpose, respite, sharing, and support. Of these, the two most important words are meaning and purpose. If you do not have something that you intend to do with your life after surgery and a reason for doing it, the road to recovery can be very long and very bumpy.

If you do not have good luck, the road to recovery will be bumpy. If you don't work at it every day, the road to recovery will be bumpy. If you try to do it all alone, the road to recovery will be bumpy.

In my case, I was determined to tell the story of my experience in a grateful way. When I was alone with my thoughts in the Step Down Unit and throughout the first two months of recovery, that is what I dreamed about, that is what I thought about, that is what I planned.

I was fortunate. I had vehicles for telling the story: our television series, *Windsor Park Stories*, and our website, The Windsor Park Theater. Neither Kitch nor I had any idea what it would take to make this happen. That's what dreaming is all about, the idea and the goal never the inconvenience.

We had to attend to hundreds of important details including fundraising, logistics, scheduling, and preparing transcripts for each episode. We invested nine months of our life recording interviews and scenes for our *Heart Scene* series. We recorded two open-heart procedures and dozens of other hospital scenes. We wrote press releases, weekly newsletters, and almost 100 articles about people, places, and events that were central to our journey of discovery and recovery.

We logged more than 3,000 hours in our editing suite laying out the timeline, checking for factual accuracy, and refining every scene for twenty-one episodes. With that done, we prepared each episode for The Windsor Park Theater.

It was the most intense and rewarding work we have ever done. It produced the most positive response to anything we have ever produced, and it continues to fill-in-the-blanks and give hope to people who are awaiting the surgery or recovering from the surgery.

A case in point—yesterday I received a call from a woman whose son-in-law had the surgery two months ago. She wanted to know about the *Heart Scene* series. After our conversation ended, she gave her son-in-law my telephone number, and he called. We talked about things open-heart patients talk about: aches, pains, medications, fatigue, and fears. I gave him the website for the Windsor Park Theater, and we agreed to stay in touch.

Later in the day, I received this note:

> **Tony,**
>
>   I think what you did here is wonderful. I only had time to look at two segments yesterday, but I want to go back and watch all of them
>
>   Let me know when your book and DVD come out. I would like to get both.
>
>   I am in WB often and would like to call you for lunch some day.
>
>   **—John**

His words were affirming and comforting on a day when I needed encouragement. You see, this series and the expenses related to the production put us heavily in debt at a time when the local economy and several of our underwriting sponsors are no longer able to support our work. It is a scary time, but, if given the opportunity to do it all over again, we would do it in a heartbeat. No pun intended.

John and I will meet for lunch, and we will develop a friendship as we both make our way along the road to recovery.

My first steps on that road took place on a brilliant June afternoon. Clutching my bright red Hug-a-Heart pillow I walked 232 steps from my room to the end of our driveway and back. Kitch was at my side. The next day I managed to walk 376 steps from my room to the top of Windsor Park where workmen were installing a mircogarden and back.

On the third day, I walked 510 steps to the end of our property line and back. Along the way, I met some neighbors who offered encouragement and well wishes. Just hearing their voices and seeing their concern for my well-being in theirs eyes was a healing experience.

Every day I got a little stronger, and every day I walked a bit farther. Soon I was doing it alone and without the pillow.

Several times during my recovery, friends invited us to lunch, and every time we accepted. We needed to get out of the house. We needed to clear our heads. We needed to be with people who cared about us and were willing to help us.

One of our very favorite haunts is the Bear Creek Café. It's a marvelous restaurant with a wonderful menu and a welcoming atmosphere. Located a stone's throw from the Bear Creek Falls, in a building that was once the office of a lumber company and later a U.S. Post Office, it is a colorful place that cannot be described. It must be experienced.

Our friends, the Zikors, introduced us to the Bear Creek Café, and until it closed temporarily, we went there often. We never had a bad meal, and we always had great conversations. We discussed the restoration of the Vulcan diesel engine with Atty. George Spohrer on a beautiful afternoon. We accompanied a former student, Joe Haberski, there one day, and we went away with his suggestion that we nominate the heroes of Flight 93 for the Medal of Freedom. We did. We received a polite letter from 1600 Pennsylvania Avenue, but as of this day, no tangible sign of any action.

One of the best days at the Bear Creek Café was the day my sister, Mary Claire, and her husband, Jack, came to visit. The place was packed, but there was no difference in service or the quality of the food.

Another special occasion was the afternoon we spent at the Bear Creek Café with Bill Gaydos and Vince Genovese. Vince is a writer and a thinker. Bill is a poet and a most decent human being. Vince and Bill are best friends. Our connection with them resulted from a friendship that developed while Kitch and I taught Vince's son, Jason, when he was an undergraduate at King's College.

They have been visitors to our home, and they have joined us in Shanksville, Pennsylvania, for our annual visit and screening there. Bill has contributed poems to our *Changed Forever* episodes about the transformational power of the Temporary Memorial to the Heroes of Flight 93.

These people and many others are a part of what Kitch and I call our Windsor Park family. This is a group of people who provide inspiration, encouragement, and support to us every day of the week. They are friends we made during our years in the classroom at King's College. They are neighbors and visitors to Windsor Park. They are people we met while producing *Windsor Park Stories* in Cape May, New Jersey, New York City, Shanksville, Pennsylvania, Penn State University, and Lake Placid, New York.

They are grandparents who are raising their children's children, and people who attend and perform at our annual Irish Teachers Festival They are people who entered our life in New York during our years as an internal video vendor at J.P. Morgan. They are the welcoming people we met at Misericordia University. They are a diverse group of people who are the threads of our life.

These are the people who held us up during the difficult time of recuperation and recovery. They are the people who wrote to us, visited us, and helped us maintain the gardens. They were always ready to lend a helping hand, offer a kind word, or lift our spirits with an act of kindness. They never judged us or expected anything from us in return. They never waited for us to ask them to help us. They volunteered, and no job was too big or too small.

People recovering from open-heart surgery need to be con-nected to neighbors, friends, and family. They need to accept their help when it is offered, and to reach out to them if it is not.

Many believe that what a patient needs is rest and solitude, and there is truth in that, but recovery is not something a patient can do alone. A kind word, a kind act, a pleasant visit, an unexpected surprise makes the process so much more tolerable.

There's a story from the production of the movie *Steel Magnolias* that applies here.

Steel Magnolias is a great friendship movie with a wonderful back story about friendship. Apparently the director was giving Julia Roberts a very hard time on the set. She was young and inexperienced. As the story goes, it did not go down well with Sally Field, Olympia Dukakis, Daryl Hannah, Shirley MacLaine, and Dolly Parton. They told him to back off, or there would be consequences. He did. The work went on, and Roberts won an Oscar for Best Supporting Actress.

For me, this is the quintessential friendship story. It involves loyalty, trust, and courage. It's a story about the goodness of the human heart. These actresses desired the good of their friend for their friend's sake. On the other hand, Miss Roberts must have been overwhelmed by their action. It must have brought her great joy. It certainly guaranteed her security and peace of mind. Five seasoned actresses stood up for their friend in a business not know for its altruism. There is nothing shallow or craven about this story.

It resonates with me on a number of levels, and it provides an insight into the healing power of friendship. During a frightening experience like open-heart surgery, this is the kind of friendship both the patient and the caregiver need and want. They hope they will have people in their lives who will look beyond the day-to-day problems associated with recovery: mood swings, mistakes, misjudgments, bouts of anxiety, depression, and exhaustion that result from a feeling of dependence and the sometimes slow period of rehabilitation.

The immortal Cicero tells us that friends do not wait to be asked, they just do what is good for their friends. There is no hesitation in friendship, it is about action. There is no question that our friends did that for us, and we are forever in their debt.

As helpful as friends are, the patient and the caregiver must must look for ways to help themselves. They must resist the temptation to shut out the world and withdraw to the security of home. The way I see it, isolation, retreat, and encampment is not a good strategy for recovery. One must get out of the house and get into the light as it were. It's not as easy as it sounds. It's much easier to stay at home and feel sorry for yourself. Kitch and I were determined not to fall into that emotional trap.

Our first major excursion, I like to call it our first date, took place the evening Maya Angelou visited Misericordia University. It was just what the doctor ordered. It was a happy event, an informative event, a wonderful event filled with emotion, drama, and a celebration of beautiful words arranged in a very special way by a beautiful woman with a heart of gold.

Sitting regally in the center of an elevated platform stage, the Poet Laureate of the World sang, whispered, bellowed, and read words of peace, joy, reconciliation, and good will. She told us she brought everything she knew with her, and she hoped that we brought everything we needed with us.

She did, and so did we. It was a a magical evening of happiness and healing.

Her message of kindness, thoughtfulness, responsibility, and caring touched our hearts in a very special way. She urged the students in the audience: "To be giving, courteous, and respectful...to dare to be merciful, just, and loving."

She captured the attention of everyone in the room with the nine words that followed: "You cannot be any of these things without courage." It was a message they and we needed to hear. Without even knowing it, this woman with the soul of an angel helped us to look forward to a new day and to our new life.

Another night out took us to the Dietrich Theater in Tunkhannock, Pennsylvania, to hear Mike Lewis in concert.

The Dietrich Theater is a monument to everything that is admirable about small town America.

This historic building, built in 1936, was saved from the wrecker's ball by a group of public-spirited people who had courage, vision, determination, and a dream. They wanted it to become a cultural center. Today it is that and so much more. It is one of the treasures in our part of the state.

Kitch and I went there to celebrate a friend: someone who entered our life several years ago, someone who has filled our life with wonderful moments of conversation, creative partnership, kindness, and genuine friendship.

On this night, we were front row center to watch a master of lyrics perform his music at a benefit concert.

Quite honestly, the evening was simply wonderful. The performers were at the top of their game:

Erin Canedy, a eighteen-year old high school senior, whose special renditions of popular songs and Broadway classics brought applause and cheers from a very receptive audience. My personal favorite was "Where the Boys Are."

John Baldino, a vice president of digital media at a local newspaper and a local bon vivant sang, danced and talked his way through his duties as emcee of the event.

Martin Young and Peter Young, two musicians extraordinaire, traveled from Nashville to bring depth and substance to the performance.

The evening, however, belonged to our friend, Mike Lewis. Mike is a talented and respected broadcast journalist. With the help of Steve Gibson and Gene Cotton, he produced three CDs in Nashville. He is a masterful songwriter and a natural performer. No matter what the situation his reaction is always the same, comforting, relaxing, and reassuring.

His duet with Erica Leigh, an accomplished singer and songwriter with one Nashville produced CD to her credit, was one of several high points during the evening. Although this was their

first performance together, you would have thought they had performed "All I see Is You," a hundred times before.

Only one word can accurately describe their moment, magical.

It was two hours of peace, calm, relaxation, and wonderful en-
tertainment. Little did we know that in that historic building on
a damp and rainy night in March, we would take the first step on
a journey of friendship with Erica Leigh and her husband, Bucky,
that would lead to the title of this book.

Three months later, in June, Erica joined Mike Lewis and Erin
Canedy on stage at Misericordia University for our Celebration of
Life Concert. It was a fitting ending to a marvelous day of friendship and confraternity with the people who helped us during our
journey of recovery and discovery.

One of the selections Erica sang that evening is a beautiful
song entitled, "Better Place, Tammi's Song." It celebrates the life
of her sister who lost her battle with cancer. The opening lyric is
poignant and powerful:

> Step inside my heart and take a walk.
> There's a thousand ways you can make it across.
> Through the deep blue colors of my youth,
> You'd find me searching for the truth.
> She wasn't just a sister to me.
> She showed me how to live life fearlessly.
> She followed nothing but her heart.
> And the day I heard it tore mine apart.
>
> Tammi, I know you're with me
> Cause I can almost see your face.
> And even though I want you here,
> I know you're in a better place.

The first line of Erica's song: "Step inside my heart and take a walk," was the inspiration for the title of this book, *Step Into My Heart*.

Nietzsche was right: "Without music life would be a mistake."

Every month during the year after my surgery, there was at least one event that enabled us to keep our eyes on the future. Some were pleasant and expected like the lighting of luminaries at Christmas in The Angel Garden with Kitch's goddaughter, Emma. Others were unexpected and very unwelcome like the Plavix induced hemorrhage in my nose just before my speech at the American Heart Association Gala in February and the painful frozen shoulder that resulted from the surgery necessitating physical therapy.

In June, it was our first formal tour of the gardens at Windsor Park. Almost 400 people came to the garden that day. The garden tour was Kitch's statement that we were on our way to recovery, and everything was going to be fine.

In July, we hosted our annual Irish Teachers Festival. The weather was uncooperative, and we had to bring everything into the Kennedy Room at College Misericordia. Our dear friend, Sr. Jean Messaros, and her assistant, Kim Caffrey, saved the day.

With a room full of visitors from Ireland, entertainers, family, and friends, we celebrated the teachers from Ireland who visit America ever summer thanks to the hard work of John and Peg McKeown and the administration and staff of King's College.

It was an overwhelming experience for me, and one that caught me quite by surprise. At one point in the evening, all of the anxiety, emotion, and fear resulting from the operation and the recovery came to the surface. When I saw the crowd, I welled up. When I saw Kitch, my daughter, Elena, and my grandchildren in the audience, I welled up, When I saw some of the special people in my life, teachers, students, and friends, I welled up. When Joanne Galvin with the help of Flight 93 Ambassadors, Chuck and Jayne Wagner, and Todd Beamer's best friend, Doug MacMillan, his wife, Chivon, and their son, Adam, presented the National 911 Remembrance Flag to Windsor Park, I welled up. When the Connemara Dancers gave me a heart-shaped rock for The Garden of Life, I welled up.

When I faced the audience to speak, my mind raced through all of the challenges Kitch and I faced in the years preceding the surgery, and I felt like a man on fire. Tormented by the disappointments of the past, ecstatic about the prospects of the future, it was one of the most emotional moments of my life. My heart was racing. My blood pressure was rising. My voice was quivering.

This night of raw emotion and unmasked humanness ended with smiles and hugs from two of the Irish teachers who knew the life-altering consequences of heart disease. Like only the Irish can, they shared beautiful words and beautiful thoughts summarized in this Irish saying: "May you live as long as you want, and never want as long as you live."

Kitch and I left the Kennedy Room, a place that mourns and celebrates the life of a president who inspired me and the young people of my generation to believe we could be more than we ever thought we could be, with Jackie Ross, a former student who drove from New Jersey to share the evening with us.

With Jackie at our side, we ended the day in The Garden of Life. Standing there under the moonlit sky, she asked if she could have her wedding pictures taken in this place in front of the weeping cherry tree she and her teammates gave us at the end of their senior year. It was the perfect ending to a beautiful day, and the perfect beginning of the next stage on our journey for her and us. We were honored and enthusiastically said yes. It became something to look forward to during the long months of winter. It became something to prepare for and something to write about. It was one of the unexpected joys that lifted our spirits, as we traveled the long and sometimes windy road of recovery.

It was a metaphor for all the things that preoccupied our life for the next nine months and beyond. We would give away what we have to help demystify open-heart surgery. We would give away what we have to help people who were hurting. We would give away what we have in words written on a page for those who wanted to read about our adventures, in scenes edited for our *Heart Scene* series, in images built for our virtual theater on the web, the Windsor Park Theater. We would give away what we have to family and friends who joined us in the garden, in Shanksville, and at our festivals. We would give away what we have to honor the doctors, nurses, and technicians who saved my life. We would give away what we have to have a guarantee that our second chance at life will have meaning and purpose.

In doing these things, Kitch and I found a life worth living, and we discovered deeper meaning in the trilogy that is central to everything we believe about life, and learning:

> You can't lead others until you lead yourself.
> You are only worth what you give away.
> You can only give away what you have.

This philosophy of life I first learned from Dr. Tim Lautzenheiser in 1992 at a leadership training camp. It was refined and concretized the following year during the production of a documentary entitled *Building Power and Class: The story of the University of Massachusetts Marching Band.* Since those days at the University of Massachusetts at Amherst, recording the story of Professor George Parks and his band, that trilogy formed the blueprint for everything I have done with my life, and everything I tried to teach students about the transformational power of living a life of dignity and class.

These three dictums have been both motivator and nemesis. They produced moments of achievement and times of misunderstanding. They are at the root of all my beginnings and endings since I saw them in action in a rehearsal hall called Old Chapel at U Mass. Without me even knowing it, they reentered my life in a new and powerful way in Operating Room 5 when Dr. Michael Harostock put his hands around my heart, so I could live to tell this story.

They are at the center of everything I believe. They are the reason I look forward to a productive, peaceful life of giving not receiving, of helping not taking, of growing not regressing, of optimism not pessimism, of reconciliation not alienation. They are the reason I have opened my heart to anyone who wants to step in and learn about my experience with heart disease and open-heart surgery.

Albert Einstein was right: "Only a life lived for others is a life worth living."

Recording a stand-up for our Heart Scene series with my Hug-A Heart pillow in front of the hospital

Completion of our Heart Scene series, a moment Kitch and I will remember forever

Kitch and Virginia Zikor in front of the Bear Creek Café after a wonderful lunch

Erica Leigh, Martin Young, and Mike Lewis performing at the Dietrich Theater, March 12, 2008

*The 2008 Luzerne County Heart Association Gala
was a night like no other*

*Jackie's dream is
realized in The
Garden of Life on
May 17, 2008*

*Bill Gaydos reading a poem he
wrote about the heroes of Flight 93
for our* **Changed Forever** *series*

*Mike Lewis, Erin Canedy, and Erica Leigh helped us to celebrate the
first anniversary of my open-heart surgery*

THANK YOU, MRS. ROBERTSON

Value work. But not any kind of work.
Anna Robertson Brown

Forty years ago Americans were captivated by the movie *The Graduate.* It was nominated for nineteen Academy Awards, and it was celebrated as the next best thing to sliced bread in moviemaking.

Essentially it is the story of a young, innocent, confused college graduate, Benjamin Braddock, who was put under the moral bus by an older woman named Robinson who, with cunning and guile, used Braddock for her own purposes. That is until he smartened up and saw what life was all about. Confronted with a moral dilemma, Braddock resolved it by falling in love with Mrs. Robinson's daughter, Elaine, and the rest, as they say, is history.

It should be obvious by now that the woman celebrated in this chapter is not the infamous Mrs. Robinson of *The Graduate.* It's a woman with a similar name but a very different outlook on life, Anna Robertson Brown.

In 1893, she published *What Is Worthwhile?* It's been called a timeless, inspirational work.

Do a Google search on *The Graduate,* and you get 83,000,000 hits. Do a similar search on Anna Robertson Brown, and there is precious little. Make a mistake like I have on several occasions and type in Anna Robinson Brown and you will find virtually nothing.

What you will find is this quotation attributed to Mrs. "Robinson" Brown prominently displayed on the administrative leadership page of the Volunteers of America, Minnesota, website: "Value work. But not any kind of work. Ask yourself, Is the work vital, strengthening my own character, or inspiring others, or helping the world?"

That's unfortunate, because what Mrs. Robertson Brown has to offer is priceless advice.

I first encountered Mrs. Robertson Brown in a doctor's office when I found an article about her in *Reader's Digest*. Getting to know her and her thoughts over the past few years has been a very joyful experience.

If truth be told, after I discovered this national treasure, I shared her thoughts with every class I taught. In my mind, her ideas have value in this technological era that commodifies everything, stripping the heart and soul out of the human equation, making us more technologically savvy and much less human in our outlook and our thinking. I wanted my students to know her. I wanted them to think about her ideas.

When I stood in front of my class sharing her suggestions with the help of a carefully prepared PowerPoint presentation, I thought I understood what she meant. To a certain extent, that was true. After my cardiac event and everything that followed, I developed a much better understanding of Mrs. Robertson Brown's words of wisdom.

Essentially she told her readers they have one life to live, and they should make the most of it. Nothing complicated here, you say. I agree. However, when Mrs. Robinson Brown asks and then answers her own question: "How can we accomplish the most without energy and power?" things get very interesting.

Her assumption is simple and very uncomplicated. We cannot grasp the whole of life, so we must ask ourselves: "What is vital? What may we profitably let go? How do we eliminate clutter?"

To answer these questions, she uses a very simple standard which she recorded in these words: "We may let go all things which we cannot carry into the eternal life."

Then, she suggests four ways to do this: drop pretense, drop spiritual worry, let go of discontent, and let go of self-seeking.

She tells her readers when they drop pretense they live in the moment without shams. They live essentially without putting on airs. They live a substantial life, not an accidental life of smoke and mirrors. Translated into the language of the marketplace: they don't live beyond their means, they don't live on overextended credit cards and pyramiding schemes, they don't live just for the moment.

Classifying worry as spiritual nearsightedness, she liberates us from the tyranny of the next-door neighbor. Stated in another way, she advises us to be ourselves. My mother and Anna Robertson Brown were on the same page on this life-enhancing principle.

Letting go of discontent frees both the mind and the soul. It enables one to live life without anger, jealousy, or regret. We are content in who we are and what we have, and we are able to celebrate our neighbor, her accomplishments, and his good fortune.

When we let go of self-seeking, there is no greed. We are content with what we have. We are capable of sharing it with others freely, and without expectation of reward.

With these four principles as a foundation, Anna Robertson Brown suggested some things we should keep:

1. Be wise in the use of time.
2. Value work.
3. Seek happiness each day.
4. Cherish love.
5. Keep ambition in check.
6. Embrace friendship.
7. Do not fear sorrow.
8. Cherish faith.

Someone said that brilliance and insight are always recorded in the questions we ask. This is so true of the questions Anna Robertson Brown wanted us to ask ourselves. For her, the essential question is not how much we have, but how we use it.

Mrs. Robertson Brown's questions about work were simple: Is your work strengthening your character? Is it inspiring others? Is it helping to improve our world?

When she addressed happiness, she asked us to be patient, unselfish, purposeful, strong, and eager.

When she talked about love, she told her readers that love trusts. It never nags, and it isn't tethered to time or eternity.

She understood that ambition could be self-destructive, and so she cautioned against substituting intellectual ambition for human affection.

Someone once wrote that a true friend never judges, always offers support, always picks you up.

Epicurus described friendship in this way: It is not so much our friends' help that helps us as the confident knowledge that they will help us.

The Emergency Friendship System recorded on a wonderful website, www. anvari.org, refines the definition of friendship with these beautiful thoughts:

> A friend accepts you as you are, believes in you, calls you just to say "Hi," doesn't give up on you, forgives your mistakes, gives unconditionally, helps you, keeps you close at heart, loves you for who you are, and makes a difference in your life.
>
> A good friend quiets your fears, raises your spirits, says nice things about you, tells you the truth when you need to hear it, understands you, values you, walks beside you, explains things you don't understand, yells at you when you won't listen and zaps you back into reality.

Anna Robertson Brown captured all these qualities in ten words: "It takes a good soul to be a good friend."

Kitch and I were fortunate to have the blessings of many good friends who understood our fears, valued our role in their lives, and walked with us during this difficult time. Through the dark period of anxiety and depression, they saw beyond the obvious, and they remain our friends today. They lightened our burden, and they helped to eliminate stress. They made us laugh, and they humbled us by their generosity of spirit.

Mrs. Robertson Brown's thoughts about sorrow and faith come out of the core of Christian belief that we are made for a life hereafter, and faith is essential to personal and spiritual happiness. The importance of a spiritual life complete with prayer, meditation, and good works becomes so obvious after a near-death experience like open-heart surgery. You realize that you are not the center of the universe.

When you are given a second chance at life, you become a much more grateful person. You realize there is a much greater reality than what you know, whom you know, and what you have. You begin to appreciate how central gratitude is to a joyful life. You begin to understand how central it is to the uniqueness of the American spirit.

Gratitude is an old and cherished tradition in America. President George Washington codified it in his 1789 Thanksgiving Proclamation with these words:

> Whereas it is the duty of all nations to acknowledge the providence of Almighty God, to obey His will, to be grateful for His benefits, and humbly to implore His protection and favor; and Whereas both Houses of Congress have, by their joint committee, requested me to recommend to the people of the United State a day of public thanksgiving and prayer, to be observed by acknowledging with grateful hearts the many and signal favors of Almighty God, espe*cially by affording them an*

*opportunity peaceably to establish a form of gov-
ernment for their safety and happiness.*

One month before my seventh birthday, 160 years later in 1949,
France donated a *Gratitude Train* to the United States. That was
a big deal in my house because my dad was a signal maintainer
for the Delaware and Hudson Railroad. I didn't understand the
concept of the *Merci Train,* or the symbolism of the fifty boxcars
loaded with 52,000 gratitude gifts given by the people of France
in response to America's acts of kindness carried aboard the *The
American Friendship Train* in 1947. For me, these were trains with
fancy names. I was too young to see beyond the obvious. Today I
am in awe of these magnificent acts of gratitude.

In recent years, many books have been written about attitudes
of gratitude. For a while, it was trendy to talk about gratitude. Unfortunately, trends come and go, and gratitude is much more than
a trend. It is a way of thinking, behaving, and living.

Dr. Stephen Post is the Director of the Center for Medical Humanities, Compassionate Care, and Bioethics at Stony Brook University. He believes that gratitude and other love-related acts make
us healthier. This belief is deeply rooted in years of research.

These are some of the positive things he discovered about a
grateful heart:

1. Just 15 minutes a day focusing on the things you're grate-
    ful for will significantly increase your body's natural an-
    tibodies.
2. Naturally grateful people are more focused mentally and
    measurably less vulnerable to clinical depression.
3. A grateful state of mind induces a psychological state called
    resonance that's associated with healthier blood pressure
    and heart rate.
4. Caring for others is draining. But grateful caregivers are
    healthier and more capable than less grateful ones.

5. Recipients of donated organs who have the most grateful attitudes heal faster.

In his book, *Why Good Things Happen to Good people*, Dr. Post tells his readers that gratitude has profound health effects, and he documents how gratitude and celebration contribute to good health.

As I see it, Dr. Post is absolutely right. For me, gratitude is about giving and receiving joy. It is about acts of kindness. Gratitude is about forgiveness. Gratitude is about hope and happiness. Gratitude is about maintaining a positive attitude and being thankful for the gifts we have in our life. Gratitude is an expression of genuine thanks and appreciation.

So what does any of this have to do with open-heart surgery, you ask?

It's a fair question, and one that I can answer in a word.

Everything.

Gratitude is central to every important lesson I learned before, during, and after I was told I had heart disease, and I needed open-heart surgery:

1. Sometimes you have to admit that you can't do everything you want to do, and that's OK. There's only one Superman.
2. If you don't find it, you can't fix it.
3. If you don't reach out for help, you won't get it.
4. If you can't laugh at yourself, then stay home.
5. Stress kills.
6. Connections matter.
7. To survive, you need a sense of purpose.
8. You learn a lot about life when you think you are going to die.
9. Gratitude is the gateway to freedom.
10. A compassionate heart is a healing heart.
11. Life is bumpy.
12. Disappointment is the mother of opportunity.

This awakening helped me to have hope and resolve during my midnight of fear and worry.

These simple principles about life, gratitude, and friendship were deeply embedded in the care, compassion, concern, expertise, and kindness of the people I met along my journey of discovery and recovery. They accurately describe the people who worked for more than four hours in the pre-op holding area and the operating room to repair my damaged heart. They capture the spirit of the people who cared for me in the Cardiac Intensive Care Unit, in the Step-Down Unit, the people who visited our home during my recovery, and the people who worked with us in cardiac rehab.

They describe in accurate and qualitative ways the person I first knew as my surgeon, Dr. Michael Harostock, and now I am fortunate to know as a friend.

In these words, I see the thoughtful, caring, competent acts of the hospital staff who helped me after my surgery. Their names are listed in the Acknowledgements section of this book.

I see the genuine friendship of people who looked beyond the obvious during my days of high anxiety, depression, and frustration, and I am eternally grateful to all those who cared enough to help me heal my damaged and broken heart. Their names are listed in the Acknowledgements section as well.

Ask any one of these wonderful people to identify Anna Robertson Brown, and they would not be able to do it. But watch their actions, and you see a perfect definition of everything she taught and everything I learned about life and what is important in life. They stepped into my heart. They transformed my world. They gave me a second chance at life, and they helped me become a better and a much more grateful person.

They illuminated the message of James 1:19 NIV: "Everyone should be quick to listen, slow to speak, and slow to become angry."

They verified the wisdom of Aristotle: "Our characters are the result of our conduct."

They reaffirmed the beautiful message of *Joshua* and Father Joseph Girzone: "The things of this world cannot give us peace," and "You have to realize that God is real and He does care for you."

They taught me the liberating message of the Hindu proverb: "There is nothing noble in being superior to some other man. The true nobility is in being superior to your previous self."

This is why heart disease and open-heart surgery are my new best friends. They changed my world. They made me fix my heart. They introduced me to people who helped me to mend my broken heart. They helped me to see and understand what really is important in life. They freed me from my past, and they opened a window to tomorrow. They set my course of action, belief, and behavior for as long as Providence will give me time to live my life in Windsor Park.

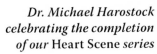

Dr.& Mrs. Michael Harostock in The Garden of Life in Windsor Park

Dr. Michael Harostock celebrating the completion of our Heart Scene series

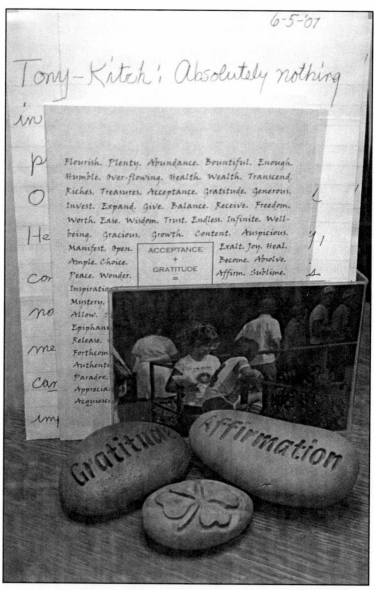

Words and symbols of faith, friendship, and life that
help me every day

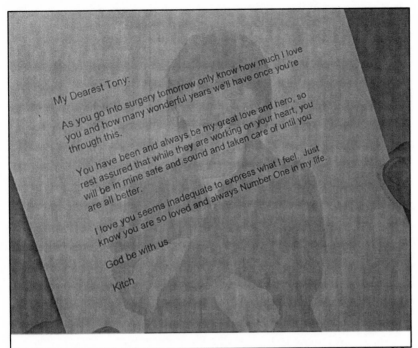

Words of hope and love from the most important person in my life

For additional information about our heart scene journey,
please visit
The Windsor Park Theater, www.windsorparktheater.com
There you will find all 21 episodes of
Heart Scene: A Journey of Discovery and Recovery

Acknowledgements

This book is an attempt to say thank you in a special way to the people who helped me during my midnight of fear and desperation. During the long days and nights before my surgery, the names and faces of family and friends were on my mind and in my heart.

During my stay in the hospital, I was blessed to have many wonderful doctors, nurses, and staff members help me. After my surgery and during my recovery, several people gave me the strength to go on. During the production of *Heart Scene: A Journey of Discovery and Recovery*, many people helped us with the production of the series, others helped us keep *Windsor Park Stories* on the air, and several performers entertained our guests at our Celebration of Life and Irish Teachers Festivals. Their names are recorded here as an expression of gratitude. Before you read them, however, I want to share a few words about a very special friend, Mike Lewis, my family and my wife, Kitch.

From the day we met, Mike Lewis and I became fast friends. We have been creative partners on a number of projects, His music is central to *Windsor Park Stories*, and he has been a frequent visitor to our home. During the good times, he celebrated with us, and during the difficult hours of life, he has been a source of inspiration to both Kitch and me. He is the person who helped us make the connection that led to the publication of this book. We are forever grateful to Mike Lewis. He defines friendship in action not words.

Some of the most precious moments of my heart scene journey were spent with my sister, Mary Claire, and her husband, Jack. My cousin and life-time friend, Cathy Pulaski O'Toole, was another positive force during this difficult time as were my Aunt Jean and Uncle Lou DalSanto and their oldest daughter, Diane Dreier. My cousin, Joseph Dreier, a medical student, called to offer advice before my surgery. My cousins, Jim Petro, Ralph Gallup, and Matthew Mussari, made contact during my recovery. My sister-in-law, Shirley Mussari, stayed in touch with Kitch for weeks after the surgery. My son, Tony, made contact by e-mail and phone. My daughter, Elena, and her husband, Jeff, did everything they could to offer help and support. "The love of family is life's greatest blessing." This proverb expresses my feelings about family in times of trouble better than any words I can compose.

For Kitch and me, 2007 was an important milestone. It marked the thirtieth year of our partnership. It began at a time when we were in the fullness of our youth. It has endured the bumps life gives all of us. Today I am more grateful for the gift of her friendship and partnership than I have ever been. Kitch is at the core of this book just like she has been at the core of everything I have dreamed about and done since the day we met. Without her kindness, encouragement, patience, support, and hard work, this book would have been just another idea that never materialized.

Whoever wrote the words: "A friend is someone who knows the song in your heart, and can sing it back to you when you have forgotten the words" provided a perfect description of Kitch. She is the music in my life.

The other members of the orchestra that made this book become a reality are:

Tom Alexander, Tina Aufiero, Vicki Austin, Mark Bailey, Roger & Beverly Barren, Louis & Helene Bigiarelli, Pam Bird, Elaine Blessing, Jeanne, Bob and Chris Boos, Brighter Light Choral Ensemble, Dr. & Mrs. Joseph Briskie, Alan Brocavich, Kay Bruzena, David Burak, Bill Coleman, Carl Canedy, Erin Canedy, Kim Cardone, Jane Carpentier, Frank Carden, Agnes & John Cardoni, Frank Cawley, Joanne Chabalko, Lori Chase, Connemara Dancers, Larry Coolick, Theresa Cope, Jen Davis, Dr. Marylouise Decker, Lou & Betty DeGennaro, Luann DeGrose, Kathy Dempsey, Joe DeVizia, Nancy Dines, Rev. Dee Donnelly, Mary Claire & Jack Doyle, Robert Drago, Diane Dreier, Donna Edwards, Judy Ellis, Dr. Jean Emilcar, Andy Ewonishon, Genny Falzone, Dr. Michael Fath, Marlene & Frank Fedak, Katy Finn, Alice Fino, Kathy Baughman Frey, Barbara Fritz, Holly Fritz Fry, Elena, Jeff, Julia & P.J. Fugate, Bill Gaydos, Vince, Gerri

& Jason Genovese, Richard Gersony, Tom Gibbon, Jan, Kerrilee & Molly Ginley, Joan Grossman, Tom Gurzynski, Joe Haberski, Atty. Barbara Hack, Jane Barton Hack, Mrs. Shirley Hahn, Janet Hall, Bob Hapeman, Rose Harlen, Dr.& Mrs. Michael Harostock, Jim Hawk, Laurie Healey, Lorraine Henry, Julanne Hogan, Jan & Mary Hoida, Dr. William Host, Robin Hurt, Gale & Robert Jaeger, Jason Jarecki, Rose & Tom Jones, Byron Joyce, Stephen Kanouse, Ruth Kemmerer, Janie Kiehl, Susan Kohut, Joan Kondzala, Ed Kopec, Audrey Kozeko, Phil Latinski, Chris Leeds, Elaine Lehman, Erica Leigh, Susan & Howard Levinson, Mike Lewis, Dr. & Mrs. Richard Loomis, Barbara Loots, Dr. & Mrs. John Lucas, Merle Mackin, Doug, Chivon & Adam MacMillan, Colleen Mahon, Jerome Maida, Julie Marvel, Judy Maxwell, Carl Mays, John McAndrew, Mark McGrane, Sean McGrath, Tom McGrath, Rebecca McHugh, John & Peg McKeown, Michelle Merkel, Sr. Jean Messaros, Jennifer Mioduski, Ellen & Jerry Mondlak, Dr. George Moses, Mr. & Mrs. Edward Mroz, Dr. Kris Nardell, Mr. & Mrs. Greg O'Brien, Mr.& Mrs. John O'Brien, Atty.& Mrs. Chris O'Donnell, Rev. Thomas O'Hara, Kathy & Brian O'Toole, Bernie Olcheski, One Laugh At Least Comedy Group, Frank Pasquini, Donna Patushny, Teresa Peck, Sr. Miriam Pfeifer, Ann Marie, Frank & D.J. Pizzani, Marianne & Nick Pokoluk, Dr. Stephen Post, Lynn Potoski, Beverly Quimby, Jim Roberts, Patrick Romano, Atty. Harold Rosenn, Jackie Ross, Daryl Rother, Michael Sackett, St. Ignatius Contemporary Ensemble, George Santee, Mr. & Mrs. Frank Scavo, Jim Schilling, Lee Sebastiani, Lori Sebastiani, Melissa Sgroi, Beverly Sharkey, Wade Shaw, Mr. & Mrs. Leonard Skibicki, John Slavoski, Dr. Linda Slavoski, Cheryl Spager, Travis Sparks, Atty. George Spohrer, Karen Stavish, Rick Stefanides, Tracy Stone, Emma Strenkert, Melissa Ulichny, Caoilfhionn & Deidre Vaughan, Chuck & Jayne Wagner, Jean & Lloyd Warneka, Marci Waymen, Rich Weaver, Bernie Wellika, Randy Williams, Sandy Wisnewski, Phil Yacuboski, Mary Ann, Joe & Jeff Yedloski, Jerry Zezza, Virginia, John & Karlina Zikor, Joe Zimak.

About the Author

Dr. Tony Mussari holds the title Professor Emeritus at King's College in Wilkes-Barre, PA. He and his wife, Kitch Loftus-Mussari, produce *Windsor Park Stories*. The series is shot in the perennial garden they created in 1996 as the outdoor set for what has become the longest running, privately owned, and independently produced television program in the history of Northeastern Pennsylvania.

Over 300 episodes of *Windsor Park Stories* have been produced and broadcast to date including a series of programs about Cape May, New Jersey, The United States Military Academy at West Point, New York, and thirty programs that document how America was changed forever after September 11, 2001.

Mussari received a B.A. degree from King's College, an M.A. degree from Niagara University, and a Ph.D. in American History from The University of Iowa in Iowa City. He began teaching at King's in 1968.

In 1970, the CEO of WNEP TV, Tom Shelburne, heard Mussari speak at a meeting in Wilkes-Barre, PA, and he invited the young college professor to become a part of the WNEP TV public affairs department.

At WNEP TV, Mussari originated and moderated the *Town Meeting of the Air* series, and he became the editorialist for the station. He researched, wrote, and presented nightly editorials for the ABC affiliate. During the Agnes Flood Disaster in 1972, he became a special investigative reporter, and he covered virtually every major story of the disaster including the Agnes Recovery Conference at the White House. Mussari was part of a team that produced several projects that won awards for the station. Mussari produced his first documentary using news department outtakes in an effort to help the victims of Hurricane Agnes.

In 1982, he and Kitch Loftus formed their own independent production company, MLA Productions, Inc. It was created to feature ordinary people with compelling stories of hope, inspiration, and service. The focus of every one of the Mussari-Loftus productions is a person telling an interesting story, not a celebrity explaining his or her story.

In 1982, Mussari and Loftus entered the PBS sponsored Matters of Life and Death competition, and they won one of thirteen grants to produce what would become one of their most celebrated works, *Centralia Fire*. This program was broadcast on PBS stations across the country, and it won several awards for MLA Productions, Inc.

Long before it was fashionable, the Mussaris eliminated the cult of celebrity from their work. They are more interested in explanation than confrontation and contention. Driven by a desire to perfect the art of storytelling, they have broadcast all of their work locally. They have never asked for or received one cent in royalties for their productions.

For more information about *Step Into My Heart,* please contact Avventura Press at 570-876-5817 or email lee@avventurapress.com

www.avventurapress.com

Printed in the United States
131894LV00003B/138/P

9 780976 155355